The History of Sportswashing

David Carlton

Contents

Introduction

M ega sporting events—like the FIFA World Cup and Olympic Games—have the power to capture the attention of a global audience, even those who don't regularly watch sporting events, or keep up with current sports news. This power is often dubbed "soft diplomacy" due to its ability to unite people regardless of their personal or political background. To some extent, this can serve as a breath of fresh air in the broken, fractured world where people keep segregating themselves in so many ways. No wonder there are some people who put their hope in the idea that sports can be a medium to spread the value of peace, grow tolerance, and boost cooperation beyond borders. Unfortunately, plentiful power comes with a price.

The way sports attract media exposure, people's attention, and huge profits is often used beyond entertainment purposes. Those who hold power—such as government officials, politicians, business people, and prominent public figures—have proven to use sports in many cases to conceal bad reputations and present to the world their clean and reputable image. This is precisely what sportswashing is—and where everything becomes problematic.

DAVID CARLTON

How Sportswashing Becomes an Issue and Why We Need This Conversation

In the past few years, the phrase "sportswashing" has been brought up for discussion. Notably, the peak of the buzz emerged during the 2022 FIFA World Cup in Qatar. Multiple new infrastructures that were specially built to support this mega event, such as the mass transportation system, stadium construction, and accommodations, became the source of condemnation around the world following the deaths of thousands of migrants who worked on those projects. Along with bribery accusations, human rights issues, labor rights abuses, improper investigations, and lack of accountability, it became one of the most controversial sporting events in history.

Despite all of these illicit practices, the 2022 World Cup was notable for several firsts and managed to set some record-breaking feats, including the final having the most viewers of any men's football final in history, more goals scored than in any previous World Cup, female referees making their debut, as well as one of the highest average numbers of viewers for a World Cup broadcast via streaming. On top of that, the highly anticipated final match between Argentina and France, as well as the impeccable performances of Lionel Messi and Kylian Mbappe, were praised everywhere, up to the point where these news stories have diverted the initial discussion about all of those controversies. The dynamics of this single event—observed through media coverage, social media buzz, and real-life conversation—have proven that sportswashing tactics have been successful in shaping a new narrative among societies and absolving those who should be held accountable.

Although the terminology is more recent, the concept is as old as the first multi-sport event that served as the model for the modern Olympic games. Back in 422 BC, this event was used by Athens to give the impression to Sparta (their rival during a prolonged war) that they were in good shape—despite the fact that they had to spend a tremendous amount of money in the midst of a crisis. This seemingly unstrategic move was actually a well-calculated political gambit designed to restore credibility. Since this tactic is still employed in the modern era, it is clear that it remains useful today and for the foreseeable future.

The growing understanding of the pervasiveness of sportswashing has led people to take a closer look at the links between sports, politics, corruption, and the business sector. Due to the enormous extent of humanitarian abuses in which the hosts and parties of sporting events are implicated, this conversation is desperately needed to encourage responsible parties to be brought to justice—as well as to ensure the value of fair play and the ethics and integrity of sports can be respected. There will be serious long-term impacts if there is no serious attempt to address these issues, including their correlation to disrespecting democracy's foundational principles, which we will talk about later in Chapter 7.

Last but not least, this book will delve deeper into everything that we need to know to understand the practice of sportswashing. Starting with the fundamentals, we will learn more about why sports are always prone to morally questionable practices, how people's reactions may make this issue persist, and how far the other "washing" practices extend in the sports world.

Chapter 1

The Problems With Sportswashing and Why It Persists

A lthough the dirty practice of covering up a tarnished reputation through sports has been around for as long as organized sports games have been played, "sportswashing" is a relatively new term, having only been coined in 2015. When Azerbaijan tried to cover up its dismal human rights record by sponsoring and hosting high-profile events like the 2015 European Games, the Sports for Rights movement proposed the concept of sportswashing to describe the practice. Then, in 2018, Amnesty International resurfaced the terminology to emphasize how the Abu Dhabi monarchy was using their ownership of Manchester City Football Club to improve their negative public image.

Today, this term refers to the practice of using sports as a distraction from political scandals, propaganda to influence the use of public diplomacy, or to incite nationalist sentiment. Although there's a tendency for people to associate the Olympics and the World Cup whenever the topic of sports' soft power is brought up, the truth is that the same tactics can be utilized in almost any branch of sports.

The Vulnerabilities of Sports

Many scandals occur in professional and collegiate sports, and sportswashing is just one of them. The same issues keep cropping up despite repeated attempts at resolution and prevention. The question is, why do illegal and morally questionable practices have such a foothold in the sports industry?

In general, unlawful practices can be influenced by a number of circumstances, including but not limited to:

- possibilities to acquire popularity, power, reputation, and wealth

- the end goal being the focal point rather than the steps taken to get there (for example, winning at all costs)

- the uncertainty of the outcomes

- lack of accountability and integrity of the elite

- exceptionally high amounts of money being at stake

- environments where discretion is the norm

Those circumstances are comparable to competitive sports. Corruption, bribery, and rigging outcomes like match-fixing are all common in sports, just as what we often hear happen in politics, governmental systems, and business. In most cases, scandals that are most notorious are those in which substantial sums of money and political influence are at stake. To give you an idea, take a look at how much money is involved in the cases of Qatar and Saudi Arabia. To offset the massive expenditure of approximately $220 billion on new infrastructure in preparation for the 2022 World Cup, Qatar relied heavily on low-wage, highly exploitable migrant labor.

However, more than 50, both individuals and business defendants, have been legally charged as a result of the investigation by the US Department of Justice (DoJ) into bribery and money laundering. Since then, the DOJ has frozen the assets of former executives who profited from the corruption case to the tune of about US$201 million. On the other hand, an estimated $1.5 billion has been spent by the Saudi Arabian government in an effort to improve its long-standing human rights violations through prestigious tournaments such as chess, golf, and horse-racing. The Saudi Cup, for example, is the wealthiest race in the world where $60 million is spent, with a $20 million prize pool.

This profit-oriented mentality also comes from the fact that sport has grown a large fan base ever since it became a mere moneymaker as part of show business. It no longer functions as a medium to preserve the idealistic image of athletics as an unadulterated pursuit. To some extent, the lack of integrity and transparency has led to many things, like protecting trade secrets or illicit deals with high-profile parties under wraps to avoid detection.

The Metaphor of Sportswashing

The "washing" part of "sportswashing" refers to the practice of covering up negative or embarrassing information, such as instances of abuse of power and financial crime involving sports executives, politicians, or corporations.

This metaphor and its meaning have evolved in recent years. At first, it was focused mostly on corporate entities and their attitudes. A short time afterwards, the term's scope widened to include governmental bodies. These shifts demonstrate how the period of accelerating global capitalism and digital innovation has prompted a wider variety of non-profit entities to prioritize reputational value fabrication.

Today, people in the public eye no longer rely on secrecy as a last resort for protecting their name after doing misconduct. They don't see the urgency to keep the facts hidden for as long, and instead, choose to draw parallels between their association (whether it's a nation, a corporation, or a sports governing body) and things that are generally viewed as favorable like certain events or activities.

Because of this transition, sports have become increasingly important to those with shattered histories and are attempting to rebuild their track records. They can use this tactic to win over influential people whose support will be invaluable in the long run, such as government officials, business leaders, or ordinary citizens.

Reasons Behind This Polarizing Issue

Apart from the tangible danger, many are skeptical about whether the strong winds of the sportswashing debate have a tendency to favor the

West and will be able to influence the government's stance on the accused misconduct.

Sportswashed Societies' Perspectives

There are massive potential benefits to the economy and the quality of life for residents of the host country when a major sporting event is held there. Since the host country won the bid and preparations began well in advance of the event's actual date, a large number of new jobs will be created in industries like construction and real estate, which will enhance economic growth and help alleviate unemployment. During the event, millions of spectators are expected to visit the venues, and they will most likely take advantage of the area's tourist attractions as well, resulting in massive profit for the tourism industry and establishing the area's long-lasting global reputation as a desirable tourist destination. Moreover, the presence of VIP guests, such as government leaders from other countries and prominent business persons, will open up more opportunities for future investment.

Not only could the host country's economy benefit from increased attention, but so could their local sports teams and leagues if they were to receive more international spotlight. As a means of bolstering youth empowerment and social development, this might pave the way for a subsequent investment in the form of assistance required to construct a high-quality future generation of athletes from that country. This can be a medium to bring equality to wider countries, especially if the host country is from a non-western region that does not often have many prospects or exposure to participate in prestigious international-level sporting competitions.

It's not surprising that firm support flows from local residents amidst the heavy criticism and accusation of sportswashing strategy. In the case of the 2022 World Cup in Doha, people in the Middle East welcomed that event wholeheartedly, as can be seen from the strong atmosphere of ecstatic crowds cheering their beloved teams. Apart from all of the promising economic benefits, having a chance to witness the championship that has always felt too far away, out of reach, and too expensive to see in person, becomes something special for Arab supporters. In addition, some locals believe that breaking a record as the first Middle Eastern country to host the World Cup can be an opportunity to break some negative stereotypes in the West regarding their country and the Gulf region in general by demonstrating to foreigners that Qataris are individuals who appreciate tolerance and harmony with anyone.

Protests and movements to boycott the 2022 World Cup were deemed unfair and misguided, despite the human rights abuses against migrant workers. There were many who contend that these kinds of illegal actions have little to do with the sport itself and that they ought to be punished on a level that is more related to politics and international law instead.

Are Those Who Have a Bad Reputation Bothered by It?

Amidst public scrutiny, along with blatant confrontation from Western media and human rights activists across the globe, real changes from respected governments don't always come in the way people expect them to. Oftentimes—if not always—the responsible parties don't really give the answers and logical explanations needed to address the sportswashing allegations. Even if they make public statements, they will almost certainly highlight the benefits that the local people can derive from those events in order to avoid the real issues.

This can be seen by the reactions from Saudi Arabia's and Qatar's authorities. After Saudi Arabia expressed their interest in double bidding to host the World Cup in 2030 and the Olympic Games in 2036, the authorities objected to the public's allegations of using sportswashing in this ambitious plan. They dodged this by asserting that Saudi Arabia is making strides in the direction of a better society and a future-proof nation—claiming that athletes and sports in general will gain from these events.

In some other cases, more blunt denials are made, even slamming back at the journalists. Human rights advocates have criticized the chief executive of the Qatar World Cup, Nasser Al Khater, for declaring in an interview that "death is a natural part of life—whether it's at work, whether it's in your sleep," in reference to the death of their migrant worker at the tournament site (Ingle, 2022). In his defense, he denied the accusations toward Qatari authorities, even expressing his disappointment on why journalists had been more preoccupied on the worker's death in the middle of the World Cup by claiming it's a false narrative.

Looking at this pattern—not only in the sense of how they respond to the accusation but also their reluctance in doing proper investigation—it's not surprising that many are skeptical on whether blowing up this issue is enough to drive significant differences. People are conflicted over this as well; some have argued that at the very least, strong media exposure can force the more neutral, independent bodies to do investigations and press charges where necessary.

Investigations like this have happened before—such as the indictments against several of FIFA's top executives by the DoJ on charges of Russia and Qatar buying votes to secure the 2018 and 2022 World Cups. Heavy exposure may be expected to drive people's sentiment toward the event

DAVID CARLTON

itself, which may lead to a possible disruption toward billions of dollars in profit. On the other hand, some have countered this by pointing out that many sportswashing cases take place in less democratic nations wherein citizens' freedom of speech may be limited and repressed. Therefore, the degree of pressure from abroad (in this case, Western media) could not be indicative of the dynamics within the country itself. It's possible that the government's reluctance to seriously examine the accusations is influenced by the fact that the critics' concerns aren't something that's widely discussed internally and that not many people are fighting for. The clear similarity between the number of scandals that are never properly dealt with in court, and those individuals actually sentenced, is one piece of evidence why media bombardment related to sportswashing accusations doesn't always result in systemic changes.

Allegations of Bias Against Non-Western Countries

Apart from the mounting evidence about illicit behavior that followed the accusation of sportswashing by certain countries or entities, one critique of this pejorative term is the fact that most of the blame has been placed on a small spectrum of non-Western entities, with the most noteworthy being Saudi Arabia, Qatar, China, and Russia. We need to apply the phrase to other regions of the world where it is prominent if we want it to have any meaningful influence and not simply be a media jargon that may provoke further tension between Western and non-Western cultures.

This may have been seen in the Olympic Games that were held in London in 2012. It could be argued that it involved a former colonial power trying to improve its reputation, influence, and power on an international stage. Thus, it is fair to wonder if this event also employed the sportswash-

12

ing method. Nonetheless, at the time, popular British narratives and their reinvention as a flourishing and progressive country were at the forefront of publications and media coverage.

How Does It Work

A variety of techniques can be used to accomplish the intended end result in sportswashing. For state leaders, owning a major club or hosting a major event like the World Cup may be a way to send out a series of messages that boost their reputation and are heard by a large number of people over a long period of time, despite the fact that these leaders are competing with the conflicting narratives from the rest of the world in the global information society. One simple way to do this is to flood negative internet search results with enough relevant and substantial content to dominate the first page of web browsers. For many people, who may not pay too much attention to social issues, it's unlikely that they will check into human rights concerns in Qatar if the top page of search results for "Qatar" is all about the World Cup. This may result in less people paying attention to the questionable moral stance behind the event and more people starting to associate the sportswashing agent in a positive light with a sport they enjoy.

Up until the point when most people prioritize the sports event for the sake of pure entertainment and enjoyment, the moral wrongdoing is minimized in a similar but distinct way. When misconduct is downplayed, it doesn't necessarily mean less people will notice or care. Instead, it makes the infringement seem less urgent, less extensive, or less essential by altering the informational context in which it is brought to people's attention. And even worse, sportswashing can make the immoral act look like business as usual. As a result, this can affect how many people are aware of or prioritize addressing the moral breach. The impact depends on whether or not audiences in general realize the moral breach.

There are at least two distinct mechanisms by which this scenario may occur. First, fans often have deep, personal connections to the teams they support and the experiences from attending match games. There may be a "halo effect"—a form of selective perception in which we give more weight to a specific area in order to positively influence our impressions of a person, event, company, or brand—if such things are associated with the owner of a well-known team or the organizer of a widely-attended event.

The sportswasher's favorable association with the moral transgression in question may have such an impact on fans that it modifies their perception of it. People are more likely to recognize and appreciate another person's positive traits if they already hold a favorable opinion of them due to their public presence. As an analogy, it's possible that when we already praise an artist for their wonderful works despite the fact that they've done some seriously immoral things, we'll end up seeing their immorality in a more positive light (or deliberately ignoring completely). Sports leagues, teams, and tournaments are no different. Owners and sponsors of successful teams may benefit from fan celebrations.

Apart from establishing a reputable image, sports and athletic events are also frequently used as a means of fostering and defining a certain type of community. Attempting to influence an individual's behavior in response to a moral transgression is rarely effective when sportswashing is the goal. Instead, sportswashing spreads because it's a medium through which people can readily communicate, organize themselves into groups, display their solidarity, and reinforce their feelings about one another. To some extent, this involves "infiltrating" the neighborhood. The sportswasher's goal is to become a well-liked and respected member of a certain sports community through active participation in that circle. Because of this, those individuals may also experience the feeling of inclusiveness; in which members of the sports community see them as one of their own and are more likely to defend, excuse, and justify them when they are criticized by people they perceive to be on the outside. The experience of defending a player's or manager's behavior, when it's obvious from an outsider's perspective that they committed misconduct, is something that all sports fans can relate to.

Despite the fact that this murky strategy can mimic various seemingly harmless behaviors, to say that any involvement in sports is sportswashing is a broad generalization. Our sports, teams, and events can be morally contaminated in countless other ways, which is quite unfortunate. Thus, it is prudent to treat any deviations from the norm with considerable skepticism and treat them as potential examples of sportswashing.

Just as sportswashing isn't the same thing as sports diplomacy or soft power in general, neither is it a synonym for either. It's important to note that sportswashing isn't just about improving public perception; it's also a means of fixing a moral issue that's conflicting with the value and moral compass of sports itself. Thus, while almost every country may cultivate soft power, and many of them build their image through sport, only some are rightly accused of committing sportswashing. These are the states whose involvement in sport is intended to distract away from, minimize, or normalize an injustice for which they are responsible and which, because it is visible to others, presents a reputational problem to be solved.

What Makes Sportswashing Specifically Associated With the Bidding Process?

Even if there are different ways to engage in sportswashing, it seems that any bid procedure is prone to being exploited to hide a country's poor standing abroad. There are extremely high chances for those who are involved to commit bribery, corruption, and other forms of misbehavior—but the question is: why?

To begin, it costs a huge amount of money to host a major international event. Despite the fact that the funding typically originates from taxpayers, the beneficiaries are not limited to citizens of the country in general or the local residents in the impacted regions. Private consultants, construction firms, government confidantes, investors, and sponsors are just some of the business people and organizers who played a part in making the event a success. This can be seen in Brazil's hosting of the World Cup in 2014. More than $15 billion was spent on infrastructure and other preparations to accommodate thousands of visitors from all over the world, including players and fans. To help fund the infrastructure, youth and women's empowerment in football, and other health-related initiatives in Brazil, FIFA established the World Cup Legacy Fund with $100 million. On the other hand, according to FIFA's financial report for 2014, their revenue was $4.8 billion while they spent only $2.2 billion.

With many people having a vested interest in this vast amount of money, and in the absence of close oversight from third parties, it is simple to succumb to corruption in order to reap even greater riches. Beyond the publicity and the chance of boosting tourism, many well-functioning democracies, autocracies, and corrupt quasi-democracies are interested in hosting such events for a variety of reasons. These include to establish a friendly and more positive image on the international arena, to enhance diplomatic leverage in regional blocks, to facilitate domestic (and sometimes international) propaganda, and to channel profitable funds to well-connected corporate interests.

Another reason is that the organizations that manage these events and select the hosts, like FIFA and the IOC, have monopoly power and are able to collect vast amounts of money from the bidding process. Although some of this funding comes from questionable sources, legal concessions are made straight to the groups. As a result of being in charge of lucrative hosting contracts, administrators at these institutions may face intense pressure to abuse their position for personal gain. Aside from their basic pay, they also get a lot of extras, like expense accounts, flights, hotels, and nightlife entertainment. Their already luxurious lifestyle is bolstered by bribes.

Both the IOC and FIFA have started putting certain changes into place to try to better regulate these practices. Since 2017, the IOC has modified its model of collaboration with a host nation to include prevention of corruption and attention to human rights issues. The last Olympics, before these rules were instituted, was China's 2022 Winter Game. France (2024 Summer Olympics), Italy (2026 Winter Olympics), the United States (2028 Summer Olympics), and Australia (2032 Summer Olympics) have all been selected as host nations since the implementation of the new model contract revisions.

However, academics and activists have their doubts about the efficacy of these model contracts for several reasons. The most significant weakness of this amended version is that it still doesn't call for independent oversight and the lack of a solid mechanism for action in the event of noncompliance.

If a member of FIFA is found to have violated the organization's Code of Ethics (which includes financial fraud like corruption), FIFA may expel them from the organization and inflict penalties, including a fine of more than $100,000 and a five-year ban from any football-related activities. In recent years, FIFA has hired a Chief Compliance Officer, appointed PwC as its auditor, and made disclosures on executive salaries. Many FIFA executives who have been accused of corrupt behavior still hold influential positions, strengthening the belief that corruption is still a major issue in the organization.

In the opinion of many specialists, corruption will remain the most pressing issue as long as FIFA and the IOC do not take stronger measures to address it. There are at least two options that can be explored. To begin, let's discuss issues related to punishment. The punishments handed down by sports governing organizations to officials who commit financial fraud ought to be significantly increased. Among these are stricter anti-corruption regulations and sanctions, as well as permanent bans for the most egregious offenders. The affluent and politically connected individuals who control the leadership of international sports organizations may only be deterred by the threat of severe consequences.

Secondly, about setting up competent administration. As with the front office or league office of major professional sports teams, the process for selecting host countries should be managed by dedicated professionals working full-time. This is crucial to reducing the potential for bias that could arise if influential, semi-retired citizens were given these positions. Appointing professionals to positions of trust increases the likelihood that such individuals will be less likely to accept bribes, as doing so could result in the loss of a lucrative employment opportunity and the associated reputational and social capital.

THE HISTORY OF SPORTSWASHING

Instead, under the existing structure, when being on the host selection committee is akin to a bonus position with extra advantages, such reluctance is unlikely to arise. People in positions of authority are more prone to try to profit from their position by buying and selling votes, albeit this is not always the case. These two measures would build on the progress made by FIFA and the IOC, and help to ensure that the spirit of fair play and competition is reflected not only on the field, but also in the boardroom and managerial level, even if it may be impossible to completely eliminate corruption risks in the bidding process.

It Doesn't Have to be the Government

It's possible that the alleged "sportswashing agent" isn't a country at all. There are a variety of ways in which it could be connected to a state, or it might have no connection at all. Of all non-state actors, big corporations stand out as the most likely to engage in the practice. Companies may also be accused if they purchase stadium naming rights to obscure, minimize, or "normalize" their role in unethical or illegal activities. Like states, companies that have committed any misconduct may try to address these issues through sporting events. People have thought for a long time that states with official obligations to protect human rights are more likely to be involved in sportswashing because they are in a unique position to break those rights. Unfortunately, it appears that businesses can also be legitimately accused of sportswashing by misusing their financial power to create new narratives that favor them.

Most experts agree that individuals rarely engage in sportswashing since the kind of reputational worry that sportswashing resolves typically necessitates some sort of relationship to a larger, collective organization, like

19

DAVID CARLTON

a firm or state. However, it's not unusual for owners of sports clubs to have poor moral records and try to mask that by publicly promoting the fact that they own a team—like the former owner of Chelsea FC, Roman Abramovich. Things about him, his profession, and his fortune that he would wish to hide, downplay, or make look like nothing are related to big businesses and the Russian government.

Acquiring a club or event isn't the only way to engage in sportswashing. It might also include non-traditional approaches to engaging with sports. This may occur if a dictatorial government constructs extensive public sports facilities. It's not limited to just television commercials; sportswashing can occur in other forms of marketing as well. Russian energy giant and government-held enterprise Gazprom was a major supporter of UEFA until recently. However, Gazprom's sponsorship was not like traditional forms of advertising because the corporation doesn't sell consumer goods. It's possible that the term "sportswashing" is more apt than discussing the various forms of profit that would ordinarily be the purpose and value of advertising.

Sportswashing requires a lot of strategic planning, which can be challenging. There is no guarantee that the period between coming up with an idea and really putting it into action will allow for the strategic use of sports. It was in 1966 that Argentina was selected to host the 1978 World Cup, but it wasn't until 1976 that the military dictatorship came to power. The idea to hold the event did not originate with the regime. Nonetheless, they made an effort to rectify the situation.

Trying to promote your country as a tourist destination is not sportswashing in and of itself. The dictatorship's ruthless and atrocious repression of dissent, including the forced disappearance of dissidents, lends credence to the theory that the 1978 World Cup was staged to distract from the regime's human rights abuses. The dictatorship hoped that a World Cup victory would unify the country and make its citizens happy, although it had to involve brute force to eliminate opposition. The dictatorship may not have intentionally hosted the World Cup in order to "sportwash," but the fact that they had to do so nonetheless provides an odd example of the strategic use of sports by the regime.

Chapter 2

The Prominent Cases

As we've already seen, sportswashing can take many forms and is not limited to hosting major sporting events like World Cups and Olympics, sponsoring tournaments, and acquiring sports clubs. Aside from football and multisport events, other sports such as golf, Formula 1, boxing, and basketball can be used to whitewash anyone's bad reputation as well.

Promoting Fascism in the 1934 Italy World Cup

The use of football tournaments to shift grave human rights violations and political strife into a more acceptable image to the international community has existed since the second World Cup ever held. In 1934, Italy was appointed to be the host country after the only other contender who bid for the same spot, Sweden, pulled out of the running at the last minute prior to the voting process. It was speculated that this decision had something to do with intimidation and bribery by loyalists of Benito Mussolini—a fascist regime dictator who was the leader of Italy at that time—as well as the Italian Football Association's guarantee of Italia's selection as host nation. During his rule starting in 1925, Mussolini gained notoriety for using assassination or other forms of disappearance to silence his critics—including political opponents and citizens—and shape public opinion in his favor.

As a means for propagating fascist ideology, the *Il Duce* (a Latin phrase that translate to "The Leader" in which Mussolini referred to himself) utilized this event to further his political agenda and exert control over the media to demonstrate to the rest of the world how effective and productive his fascist civilization could be. To support this vision, the presence of fascist symbols could be seen everywhere, from its official poster to postage stamps that covered Italian stores and streets, including illustrations showing Hercules standing over a football with his arm raised in a Nazi salute. The controversy and speculation didn't stop there. His authoritarian approach made it possible for him to control how the media broadcast the game. For example, he ordered the radio commentator to repeatedly praise the large crowds at the stadiums, regardless of what really happened there. Due to the fact that certain referees made rulings that were biased in favor of the Italian team, it led to rumors that Mussolini had a hand in choosing the referees.

The 1936 Berlin Summer Olympics Games, Germany

The 1936 Summer Olympics are notorious for the way Adolf Hitler utilized them to glorify the Nazi ideology, making them one of the most infamous Olympics in history. Unlike other more recent sporting events where those with tainted reputations are the ones who make decisions to bid to be the host country, Germany was chosen to be the host two years before the Nazis came to power. Although it's unknown whether or not Hitler himself wanted to host the Olympics since he wasn't really into sports, he eventually took his Minister of Propaganda, Joseph Goebbels, at his word that it would be an opportunity to showcase the ideals of the Aryan race and the "new Germany" that had been created under Nazi control.

Albeit the genocide wouldn't happen until years later, there had been a lot of violence directed towards non-Aryans, including the refusal of Jewish athletes to join Germany's Olympic national team. It was inevitable that a wave of protests would occur in response to this ill-treatment of non-Aryans, especially after the Nuremberg Laws were enacted in 1935, which drastically altered the lives of German Jews by stripping them of most of their basic rights. As a result, the international community called for boycotts to discourage countries from sending their athletes to participate—making it the first boycott effort in Olympic history—and demanded moving the event outside of Germany. This pressure inspired the holding of the Popular Olympics in Spain as an Olympics alternative to demonstrate the leftist anti-fascism movement, a month before the opening of the Nazi Olympics. More than 6,000 athletes and roughly 20,000 spectators from across the world were scheduled to attend this alternate event despite the lack of perks and frills present compared to the official tournament; however, the event was ultimately halted due to the Spanish Civil War.

Hitler had several strategies in place to ensure his propaganda got across while putting down big controversies. He invited a bunch of prominent people, including businessmen, journalists, and politicians, to attest to the fact that Germany was a peaceful, welcoming nation to everyone. The Nazis were even willing to go the extra mile to pull off a political stunt by inviting Helene Mayer, a widely regarded part-Jewish female fencer who won a gold medal in fencing at the 1928 Olympics, back onto the German Olympic team. Quite similar, a half-Jewish Theodore Lewald was appointed as an "advisor" to Germany's Olympic Organizing Committee—though this position was most likely only for show.

If on a normal day the slogan "Jews Not Welcome" was easy to find everywhere, Goebbels ordered that those signs be removed from Berlin streets during the 17 days of the Olympics. Hitler also promised to maintain the stability of the city by dispersing anti-Semitic rallies. As a replacement, the five-ring Olympic flag was put up in every building in the city, public spaces, and sporting venues as if they truly believed in the flag's philosophical value in cooperation with five continents across the globe. In spite of this, the swastika flag and the "Heil Hitler" salute could be seen in every corner of the city throughout the games. When the time came to announce and give the medals to the winners of every sports branch, Hitler always seemed to enjoy rewarding or congratulating Aryans' German, Finnish, or Italian winners; yet the same thing never happened when the winners were black or any other non-Aryan athletes.

On top of that, there was still one more propaganda strategy that was arguably the reason why the Berlin Olympics are so memorable. Hitler commissioned German filmmaker Leni Riefenstahl to create a two-part documentary film called *Olympia* in order to chronicle the events visually. *Olympia Part I: Festival of the Nations* and *Part II: Festival of Beauty*, both of which came out two years after the event concluded, set new artistic and cinematic benchmarks in terms of how sports were portrayed on screen.

Riefenstahl was capable of displaying extraordinary athletic performance by using close-ups, slow-motion, and an incredible variety of camera angles. The film's opening sequence involves a whirlwind journey through space and time, beginning with ancient Greece and ending with the Olympic cauldron being lit in Berlin—the torch relay itself having been performed for the first time in the 1936 Olympics. The actual track and field competitions that took place at the Berlin Olympics are covered in the second part of Olympia.

However, behind its stunning artistic achievements and seemingly neutrality from any political overtones, there is an apparent message of Aryan supremacy and the National Socialism that they wanted to show the world. Footage of Hitler enjoying the tournament from the stands while clapping and cheering his national team whenever they did well or banging his hands on his uniformed leg was often assumed to be an intentional tactic to humanize the ruthless dictator. The film's fixation on race is also problematic. The commentator who repeatedly called Jesse Owens "the fastest man in the world" and who beamed at the camera afterward as the sole black contender to feature in Olympia, may have helped to give a positive portrayal of the four-time Olympic gold medalist who has been renowned for his impressive victory at the 1936 Olympic and reverse the propaganda allegation. On the other hand, "two black runners facing the strongest of the white race" was how Olympia's broadcaster described the 800-meter final—making it harder to dismiss the racial strife in this movie and overall games.

The 1978 World Cup in Argentina

In June of 1978, when the tournament began, Argentina was deep in the grip of its murderous military dictatorship, commonly known as the "Dirty War." It all started roughly two years before the World Cup, when military officers arrested Isabel Perón, the president who was elected democratically, and replaced her with General Jorge Rafael Videla.

Videla, a strict authoritarian, wasn't a person who enjoyed football. He thought it was boring and commonplace and only somewhat fascinating as a universally recognized icon of modernity. Despite all of that, he watched the games nonetheless. It was a driving force of pride and identity for Argentines and untold more around the world and he knew that. With the South American nation under military rule, Congress shuttered, and all unions prohibited. Only hours after taking power, Videla and his associates who plotted the coup still have the opportunity to talk about the World Cup.

Argentina's hosting rights had been granted over a decade prior, but Videla and his closest advisors saw the tournament as a useful tool in retaining their control and suppressing opposition. Winning public support at home and abroad was considered crucial for sustaining stability in the face of a distressed economy, suffering under inflation rates above 300% and armed dissidents from Marxist guerrillas known as the Montoneros.

In a few weeks, the military junta declared the World Cup a public interest, despite warnings that it could ruin the nation's finances. And despite laws from FIFA that prohibit national governments from being directly engaged in arranging the event, the Junta established a separate structure run by elite commanders to oversee the mission. With the stolen power at stake, Videla was not going to take any chances. International condemnation of the junta had grown more vociferous in the wake of the coup, with critics becoming increasingly louder, especially across Europe.

There was an increase in the disappearance of prominent Argentineans in the fields of academia, the arts, and even professional sports. Many of these people were taken by government operatives and never seen or heard from again. Surprisingly, over the course of several years, eighteen people who were all part of the La Plata Rugby Club and who were all thought to have held leftist political ideals vanished without a trace. And all the while, the severely regulated media said that the Argentine public's foes, the nebulously labeled "terrorists," had to be stopped entirely.

The French journalist and intellectual collective known as C.O.B.A. (Organizing Committee for the Boycott of the Argentina World Cup) was created in late 1977. They plotted a coordinated effort to convince the French national team, captained by the afro-sporting goal scorer Michel Platini, to withdraw from the competition. It was declared in the group's manifesto that not just France but also Italy, Scotland, Sweden, Spain, and the Netherlands should avoid joining. The official World Cup logo—two outstretched arms encircling a football—was given a somber makeover for flyers plastered all around Paris, with the addition of some imposing barbed wire.

In preparation for such coverage, the Junta had already signed the services of the American public relations agency Burson-Marsteller on a million-dollar contract to help build positive international opinion of Argentina and its government. New York account management developed a comprehensive strategy to create a fresh image based on firmness, with the World Cup serving as the focal point and the need to combat any negative news overseas as a primary motivator. When asked about the unfavorable publicity from outside Argentina, Videla dismissed it as an "anti-Argentine" organized strategy of falsehoods and disinformation.

The Junta had a stranglehold on the domestic press, and this helped them convince most Argentines that they were the victims of this falsehood and inspired them to resist. Para Ti, a women's periodical published once a week, made headlines when it encouraged its readers to write and send postcards to their foreign friends using postcards neatly embedded in the magazine's pages. Argentine military police, many of whom were under the age of 20, patrolled city streets in the months leading up to the tournament, conducted random inspections for identification documents, and sometimes accepted bribes. There were checkpoints all around the country, and passing cars were frequently detained for examination. Poor areas near essential public facilities, including airports and stadiums, were forcibly cleansed so that they wouldn't attract the attention of visitors from other countries. When Brazilian and FIFA president Joao Havelange showed up in Argentina on May 23, 1978, this country was ready to present its "perfect" image to the world.

On June 1, an opening ceremony, attended by 67,000 people, was conducted at the Estadio Monumental in Buenos Aires, which had been renovated specifically for the tournament. The inaugural match would follow on June 2. Less than a mile away from where they were standing, they could see the infamous Navy Superior Mechanics School (ESMA), a cluster of facilities where the Argentine Junta brutalized, investigated, incarcerated, and eventually murdered thousands of people. Pregnant women and their newborn babies were among those brutally abducted from their own homes and thrown from military jets into the wide Rio de la Plata, where they drowned.

The 2014 Winter Olympics and 2018 World Cup in Russia

The 2014 Winter Olympics were Vladimir Putin's first personal megaproject after the fall of the Soviet Union to prove to the world that Russia was once again a global superpower. His decision to bid on hosting the 2018 World Cup was additional evidence of his fixation on projecting an image of unrivaled might. Despite the solid allegation of bribery, the deaths of workers who were involved in building new stadiums, and other grave human rights abuses, Putin's close-knit friendship with FIFA President Gianni Infantino was seen as his golden ticket to win the bidding process. In addition to hosting two of the biggest sporting events in the world, Putin employed the state-owned Russian energy company Gazprom to sponsor UEFA and a number of football clubs in an effort to whitewash his tainted reputation.

All of this sportswashing attempt has helped Russia to establish legitimacy as a post-Soviet global superpower, only for a far more dire purpose: provoking war. This could be seen when Putin deployed soldiers to Ukraine for the first time to annex Crimea only days after the Olympics.

According to a report published in 2018 from Building and Wood Workers' International, at least 21 migrants died during the construction of new stadiums for the World Cup. Accidents involving falling from heights or heavy machinery crushing laborers accounted for the vast majority of fatalities, meaning that many could have been avoided if adequate health and safety measures were put in place.

There were at least 110 North Korean slaves and prisoners working in the Zenit Arena, one of the World Cup arenas in St. Petersburg. The facility had been plagued by financial fraud, slavery-like conditions, and the systemic exploitation of migrant workers, all at a cost of about $1.5 billion and the lives of some of those who have worked there. Many employees were not provided with equitable employment agreements, which led to a lack of fair compensation and an opaque wage-setting process. To make matters worse, they were subjected to dismal and unsanitary living quarters by their employers, and were expected to work in brutally frigid winters.

Furthermore, the lucrative sponsorship deals between Gazprom and UEFA and various football teams were not without their own set of issues. After mounting international pressure and questions on whether the €40-million-per-season deal in place since 2012 was really worth the reputational damage stemming from Russia's invasion of Ukraine, UEFA decided to end this sponsorship in February 2022. Even though this is the right thing to do, many people have said it's already too late. With the success of hosting two global events, along with all of the televised entertainment enjoyed by people across the globe, it's understandable if people believe that Russia has already gained influence and soft power.

Following the IOC's recommendation for the International Sports Federations and sports event organizers to ban the participation of Russian athletes in international competitions—to which most comply—a new debate has emerged over whether the ban is still relevant and should continue to be enforced. Some raise this discussion when considering the IOC's lofty vision to promote cooperation and peace through sports—a vision which shouldn't punish athletes for government decisions. There has been a pattern of leniency ever since Putin invaded Georgia in 2008, during the Beijing Summer Olympics. Rather than implying that Russia should be expelled for breaking the Olympic Truce, which had resulted in hundreds of casualties and thousands fleeing their homes, an IOC representative stated how the attendance of Russia and Georgia in the tournament reflected well on the value and spirit of the Olympics themselves. On the other hand, Putin's strategy to use the grandiose and contentious Beijing Olympics as a diversion from his invasion of Georgia was a calculated political maneuver—knowing that he had already secured his right to host the 2014 Winter Olympics.

The 2008 Summer Olympic Games and 2022 Winter Olympic Games in China

China's Olympic hosting in both 2008 and 2022 got off to a rocky start and ultimately left a dismal legacy. Criticism of China's attempt to wipe out Uyghur and Tibetan communities, as well as concerns expressed by human rights advocates about forced labor and the government's propensity to stifle or get rid of those who disagreed with their policies, were just the tip of an iceberg that led people to question the IOC's selection of China to be the host country. As a means of silencing these claims and evading responsibility, the Chinese government promoted the false narrative that life for Uyghurs is civilized, peaceful, harmonic, and fulfilling. In one of the joint conferences during the 2022 Winter Olympics, a Chinese government official, along with the IOC, explicitly denied any knowledge of detention centers and forced labor—the IOC spokesperson did not provide any clarification, instead implying that the points raised were neither central to the IOC nor the purpose of the news conference.

In an apparent effort to corroborate their defenses as well as their vehement defiance of Western criticism, an Uyghur cross-country skier was chosen to participate as the Olympic cauldron lighter during the opening ceremonies—lending credence to the claim that all ethnic groups were equally represented. This choice was highly politicized since it sought to justify the host country's treatment of ethnic minorities that had been suppressed under the guise of a tradition honoring individuals seen as icons of the host country's vision or sporting legacy. While Chinese state media portrayed this action as a proof of progressiveness, many Uyghurs living abroad, who have worked to bring attention to the re-education camps and widespread arrests of Uyghur Muslims, found this political circus to be deeply upsetting.

Keeping up the Olympics' carefully crafted image—or the country's reputation more generally—seemed to necessitate totalitarian government surveillance in the form of media censorship, in which the administration has complete control over what information can and cannot be publicized. Among those who were cautioned were foreign journalists and athletes, who were asked to respect Chinese law by refraining from any public comments, actions, or writings that might be seen as illegal.

The 2014 World Cup and 2016 Summer Olympics in Brazil

In 2007, it was announced that Brazil won the bidding process to be the host of the 2014 FIFA World Cup. Back then, Brazil's economic development expanded by 4.5%, inflation was under control, and the value of the currency remained steady. This marked the South American country's best economic period in decades. The duration of the economic boom seemed to show that it would last beyond a decade. And no-one predicted that the sweet-spot of all these World Cup preparations would be between the announcement of hosting the tournament and the arrival of the hideously costly competition itself.

By May 2014, it was stated that consumer confidence had significantly dropped as a result of four straight quarters of slowing economic growth from late 2013 to early 2014. This was the first time this has happened since the global financial crisis of 2008–09. By this time, Brazil was in a state of upheaval, which was ironic, given that the opening ceremony of the largest individual sporting spectacular on earth was rapidly approaching. Thousands flocked to the streets to demonstrate against rising prices for public transportation, corruption, and inequality, and most notably, the World Cup.

Hosting the World Cup, which included burning billions of dollars for the sake of six new pretentious stadiums, seemed insensitive and distant from the public's interest in a country where inflation was making it harder for people to afford basic needs and where the proportion of physicians and nurses were far from enough toward the entire population. Prosecutors from the federal government sought court injunctions preventing any more tax payers' dollars being used to cover the costs of the postponement of construction of the new infrastructures.

It is not unusual for politicians and government officials to have lofty goals in order to highlight their country's progress. However, this plan failed because of the decision of Brazilian President Lula da Silva to co-operate with one of the most corrupt organizations in the world, FIFA. An estimated US$11.7 billion was spent on World Cup preparations alone, with US$4 billion going into the construction or renovation of 12 venues. No one would be surprised if suspicions were raised regarding possible corrupt relationships between government officials and private investors given the size of this sum. Some of these stadiums were even struggling to be equipped for the tournament, let alone the massive infrastructural upgrades that were promised to locals as a perk of being the host country.

In 2009, the completion of a high-speed rail line connecting Rio and Sao Paulo was predicted for 2020, years after the World Cup. Many Brazilians were upset, feeling their government was out of touch with reality. As a result, federal prosecutors asked a court to halt the broadcast of government advertisements praising the benefits the World Cup would bring to Brazil. They argued that the promotions were completely at odds with reality.

Rio de Janeiro was again on the verge of protests and controversies prior to the 2016 Summer Olympics. Protests are commonplace for worldwide megaprojects, but authorities typically respond and resolve these conflicts in the same manner regardless of the specific nature of the protests. The Rio's organizers would take all necessary measures to ensure that the celebration goes off without a hitch. To disperse protesters outside the venues prior to the games, the police resorted to extreme measures, such as the use of tear gas and rubber bullets. For the safety of the games, not only did the Brazilian police force work with their international counterparts, but also military advisors and foreign intelligence personnel.

The funding for the Olympics was being affected by Brazil's economic crisis at the time; the worst recession the country had seen since the 1930s. To help cover costs, the organizers even looked for methods to save money on things like the food and travel expenses of Olympic officials. The financial problems were heightened by the suspension and later impeachment of Dilma Rousseff, the President of Brazil at the time, which heated up the political climate in the period. Rousseff's 2014 reelection campaign and a large corruption scandal, including bribery and price rigging, led to her being accused of breaking budget restrictions to raise spending. Corruption in Rio had a negative effect on the Games themselves. Involved in the scam were multiple large Brazilian construction companies that were tasked with building the majority of Olympic-related infrastructure.

The spread of the Zika virus, which was designated a public health emergency in early 2016, was one of several causes for concern in Brazil in the lead-up to the Olympic Games. Microcephaly is a congenital disorder in which a baby is born with an abnormally small head and has been related to the mosquito-borne virus that recently swept the Americas. Women who are pregnant or expecting to get pregnant were urged to avoid nations where the Zika virus had been detected, causing safety concerns among those who were considering attending the event in person. There was also excessively polluted water from human sewage, the cause of an alarming number of disease-causing viruses and bacteria. In 2015, some competitors got sick from taking part in test activities that used water. Rio's campaign for the Olympics included promises to enhance sewage sanitation and clean up the city's water. However, Brazilian authorities admitted that the water quality would not be as good as hoped.

Apart from the violent behaviors of the authorities and issues prior to the Olympics, another problem arose after the Olympics were over. Hosting the Olympics sparked hope for Rio and Brazil in general in terms of boosting foreign tourists' visits, opening new job opportunities, improving public safety, and integrating public mass transportation systems. All of which were supposed to be a long-term legacy that benefited local people and the nation's economic development.

Brazil established a series of public policy frameworks in the areas of culture, urbanization, mobility, environmental sustainability, and education to help reach this goal. In total, 27 projects across local, state, and federal levels were mandated by that plan in 2014. All of them had nothing to do with the Olympics themselves, but would be made easier thanks to the event, such as the construction of new transit routes. Unfortunately, not a single one of these endeavors ever saw fruition.

In total, the cost of hosting the Olympic Games in Rio de Janeiro was little over 39 billion Brazilian reals, or about $7.4 billion in current dollars. This figure included compensation paid to the people of Vila Autodromo, who were forced to leave their houses to make way for the Olympic Park. Although the government spent a lot of money on relocation and compensation, the plan didn't work out as intended, and several locals disclosed the government's severe attitude, including the use of psychological pressure, threats, and even physical assault. In addition, the Rio municipal government discontinued essential services including mail delivery, household waste management, and street lighting in order to exert even more pressure on the populace.

The Olympic Games in Brazil ended up creating more conflicts than they resolved. A lack of forethought on the part of decision-makers was the main issue. There was no coordinated effort to leave a lasting legacy. The lack of clear goals and long-term objectives from the start wasn't the only reason why the projects couldn't be a priority. In fact, they were simply abandoned when a new administration took over.

The arrest of Brazilian Olympic Committee (COB) head Carlos Arthur Nuzman, who had held the position for 22 years, only exacerbated the status quo. After being accused of bribing the IOC members to ensure Rio would be selected as the Olympic Games' host city, he was found guilty of corruption and criminal organization in 2017.

Additional unrealized goals included cleaning up and protecting the lagoon and Guanabara Bay, where the sailing contests were held. During the campaign to select Rio as the host city, the Sergio Cabral government pledged to significantly reduce the amount of garbage and sewage entering the bay by 80% by 2016. While flood management for residents near the Maracanã was ultimately implemented, wastewater treatment was estimated to be less than 40%, according to the State Water and Sewage Company (CEDAE) (Galante & Goldenbaum, 2021).

At first glance, the misuse of taxpayer funds and inability to fulfill the promised legacy seem more like indications of inefficient and negligent governance than an explicit sportswashing approach, as other non-democratic countries have done. However, the way authorities use excessive force to hide the protests and handle dissident societies that dare to question the government's policies depicts a grim reality of police brutality, a lack of accountability, and disrespect to the basic rights of civilians, especially those living in slum areas.

While this was already a serious issue expressed by humanitarian activists prior to the 2014 World Cup, it took a turn for the worse in the run-up to the 2016 Olympics. Since the 2014 World Cup, Brazilian authorities and sports governing organizations in Rio implemented violent security measures that resulted in a spike in murders and human rights violations by police forces. Instead of fulfilling the government's promise to improve public security for all civilians, the former Executive Director of Amnesty International Brazil, Atila Roque, said that at least 2,500 people have been killed by police in Rio since 2009—which was the year when the city was awarded the 2016 Olympic Games (Amnesty International, 2016). Despite this unusually high number, the authorities were reluctant to conduct thorough and impartial investigations. Many argue that the ambition to host two biggest sporting events in the world was their way to polish their failure to protect civilians and preserve human rights value by creating a false image as a safe and friendly country to the international community.

The 2022 World Cup in Qatar

Even if you're not a huge soccer fan, chances are, you probably know that there have been a number of rumors about scandals and problems since FIFA announced that Qatar would be hosting the 2022 World Cup. For a small country located in a region that isn't renowned for sports, being selected to host the biggest sporting event in the world means that they can get a whole new level of visibility. In politics, visibility provides some kind of leverage and bargaining power to influence international affairs, including making differences that eventually can give an advantage in the middle of other more powerful developed countries.

Despite the benefits of polishing their reputation, being in the global spotlight does come with a price. The more attention they get, the more the public will be educated on the negatives associated with them. It's inevitable that the host country and the sports governing organization will always be subject to severe questioning and calls for responsibility in light of the growing public awareness of the human rights and financial problems surrounding this tournament.

So, what exactly are the issues and controversies that have surrounded the Qatar World Cup that have made the public so enraged to the point that many have termed it one of the worst sportswashing examples in history?

1. Severe exploitation over low-paid migrant workers who built new infrastructures and stadiums dedicated for the World Cup

In order to accommodate millions of spectators from across the globe, the Qatar government invested roughly $220 billion to build seven new stadiums, around 100 new hotels, and a mass transportation infrastructure including the metro system, a new airport, and new roads. However, there was one sector where costs were kept to a minimum: labor.

At least 30,000 migrant workers from India, Bangladesh, the Philippines, and Nepal were hired to build all of those new infrastructures. Even without the World Cup, Qatar heavily relies on its migrant workers to ensure economic development. Until around the late 2010s, about 94% of the country's total workforce, which totaled approximately 2 million, consisted of migrant workers (Ward, 2022).

However, the government doesn't ensure that these workers will be provided with even the most basic of living standards, and their atrocious labor practices are not limited to this event. The *kafala* is a framework of sponsorship that establishes a number of legally enforceable agreements to govern the relationship between foreign employees and their host country's employers. The majority of the nations in the Gulf Cooperation Council (GCC) have adopted this model. These countries include Qatar, Bahrain, Kuwait, Saudi Arabia, the United Arab Emirates, Lebanon, Jordan, and Oman. These workers are extremely at risk under this arrangement because they are not afforded any protections under the labor law of the country in which they are employed.

Because of this, they are mostly prevented from exercising their fundamental labor rights, such as the right to become a union member or participate in a labor dispute process. The situation is exacerbated by the fact that employers (rather than the government) have greater say over their employees' legal standing, as only the sponsors can renew or terminate the employees' employment and resident visas. Despite Qatar's assertions that the system has been eliminated—for example, workers no longer need sponsors' permission to switch jobs or leave the country—many human rights activists argue that the reforms are poorly enforced and do not amount to elimination because sponsors still have an aberrant degree of control over workers' lives.

Deathly repercussions have resulted from the frantic preparations for the World Cup, worsening already appalling work and living environment that includes wage embezzlement, long working hours, and both physical and sexual assault. In 2021, The Guardian reported that over 6,500 laborers from Pakistan, India, Sri Lanka, Bangladesh, and Nepal died in Qatar since 2010 (Pattisson & McIntyre, 2021). Since these numbers don't account for deaths that took place in the latter months of 2020, the actual death toll is almost certainly far higher. There is no breakdown of these numbers by location or type of work; however, it is likely that many of the fatalities occurred on the World Cup infrastructural development. The official statement cited a number of causes of death, such as suffocation, blunt force trauma from falling, and an undisclosed cause of death from decaying. Nonetheless, the majority of them were labeled as "natural deaths", frequently owing to abrupt cardiac or respiratory failures.

It has also been brought to light that there is an absence of transparency on the specifics of these tragedies. The governments of the workers' home countries and their embassies in Doha have been reluctant to publicly divulge the data, which has prompted another suspicion regarding political motives behind the reluctance. There are discrepancies between the numbers kept by several government departments in Qatar, as revealed by an extensive review of the country's official statistics. Moreover, there is no uniform system for registering the reasons for death.

2. Dismal record of human right abuses

Human rights organizations throughout the world have condemned Qatar for decades because of its discriminatory policies against women and the LGBTQ+ community. The country's penal law contains regulations that make sexual activity between individuals of the same sex illegal. However, the law that fails to prosecute those who commit acts of domestic abuse and sexual assault is a clear indication of misogyny and extreme patriarchal system.

Additionally, a person can go to jail for exercising their right to free speech in this country. In recent years, the government has taken concrete steps to weaponize their penal code by making it illegal to speak out against the Emir, to blaspheme against Islam, or to promote "fake news" in order to stifle dissidents or punish anyone who dares challenge government policies. It's common knowledge that the government actively harasses independent journalists who go there to cover stories on the treatment of migrant workers. Wide-ranging limitations were placed on journalists by the government during the World Cup in an effort to control the narratives in the media.

3. Corruption and bribery to win the bidding process

It's natural that many fans were taken aback when Qatar was selected to host the 2022 World Cup, given the caliber of the other countries who sought to do so (including the United States, Australia, and Japan). This response was not entirely without reason. Despite the Arab world's century-long history of football, the Qatari national team has never made it to the World Cup finals. This small Gulf state lacked adequate football facilities, despite being among the world's wealthiest nations thanks to its abundant natural gas resources. Moreover, July's blazing heat would prevent the tournament from taking place when it's typically held. With all of these factors in mind, and given FIFA's dubious reputation, it's easy to see why bribery rumors have circulated.

That suspicion was confirmed following investigations into bribery of all 22 panel members who participated in the decision leading to a number of convictions (Panja & Smith, 2022). In spite of the corruption, there is still a counter-argument that see's FIFA's decision to award the 2022 World Cup to Qatar as part of a larger strategy to increase its presence in the Middle East by forming partnerships with wealthy countries like Qatar.

4. "Greenwashing" and environmental impact

Organizers of the 2022 World Cup in Qatar said theirs would be the first tournament in history to not produce any net carbon emissions. Independent environmental researchers, such as the environmental lobby group Carbon Market Watch, voiced their displeasure at the propensity for sports committees to underestimate the CO_2 emissions, believe deceptive statements, and the concrete costs to the environment.

More than a million tourists' plane rides and hotel stays produced the most CO_2 emissions. Due to a lack of available lodging in Qatar, shuttle aircraft brought fans into the desert city every day. Officials stated that they would invest in internationally recognized and certified carbon credits to compensate for the emissions that could not be avoided, such as those caused by the roughly 160 flights a day that departed from countries like Oman, Saudi Arabia, Kuwait, and the United Arab Emirates in the lead-up to and during the tournament. According to environmentalists, this is just a "greenwashing" tactic meant to divert public attention away from what had to be done to solve the climate catastrophe, which is the rapid reduction of emissions from fossil fuels. Nonetheless, the absence of clarity raises the possibility that the actual emissions from the event were significantly higher than estimated before the tournament.

There are several environmental issues besides emissions, with use of water and improper disposal of trash being other major problems. To meet their freshwater demands, the people of Qatar have increasingly turned to desalination. The process of desalination uses a lot of energy, primarily fossil fuels, to purify water so that it can be used for agriculture and human consumption. Desalination plants are problematic because they discharge hazardously hot brine into the ocean.

Brine, a saltwater solution with a particularly high concentration, is harmful to marine life in general, not just coral reefs, because it kills off the smaller marine species that make up the ecosystem. Additionally, the filters on intake pipelines can suffocate tiny marine life and force them to crash into each other, where they will suffer excruciatingly and die from the tremendous pressure generated by the machine's system. The demand on desalination was increased by the enormous water needs of running eight stadiums and 130 training areas utilized in preparation for and during the tournament. With Qatar already experiencing a severe water scarcity, adding this extra pressure is far from desirable.

The environmental impact of constructing seven brand new stadiums and renovating another was either overlooked or deliberately downplayed. Six of the new stadiums are long-term structures, while one—Stadium 974—will be dismantled. Officials estimated that Stadium 974 will emit 438 kilotons of carbon dioxide, compared to 206 kilotons for the six permanent ones (Dufrasne, 2022). Criticism of this illogical calculation arises from the fact that the six permanent stadiums have a far lower carbon output statistic than the temporary one; this raises questions about the calculation approach and the viability of the sustainability claim, not just in this case but in other environmental issues as well.

Aside from concealing these controversies, Qatar's ambition to host the World Cup is driven by its desire to develop its international reputation. Due to their own political vulnerability, it's not surprising if they need to be seen as legitimate and trusted members of the international community. In 2017, several of Qatar's neighboring countries—including the United Arab Emirates, Saudi Arabia, Egypt, and Bahrain—imposed a land, sea, and air embargo on Qatar, resulting in severed diplomatic ties and a blockade. These neighbors accused Qatar's government of supporting terrorism and Islamists in the region and of drawing closer to Iran. While denying the accusation, Qatar was adamant about maintaining the relationship with Tehran, a major trading partner across the Persian Gulf where both Qatar and Iran share a critical offshore natural gas field. Despite suffering from the blockade, Qatar leveraged its vast natural gas wealth to make its economy more self-sufficient and successfully build new trading links. Eventually, the boycott was lifted in 2021.

Acquisitions of Federations or Sports Clubs

In the modern history of English football and particularly the Premier League, there have been a number of significant events more business-related than sport. First, it's the origin myth that involves a get-together of new Thatcherite club chairmen plotting to secede for a larger portion of broadcast rights. Due to this, the Premier League was able to strike a contract with BSkyB, which resulted in increased revenue for the league's clubs. Then came the 2003 acquisition of Chelsea by tycoon Roman

Abramovich. Until Abramovich came along, no other owner in the league had ever made a billion dollars. He turned a squad that was languishing in mid-table into a serious contender for the Champions League. Then, only 5 years after this, in 2008, the dynamics changed again when Sheikh Mansour's Abu Dhabi United Group purchased Manchester City. His position as Deputy Prime Minister of the United Arab Emirates and a member of the royal family has elevated him to a status previously unknown among business owners: that of a monarch. Sheikh Mansour assumed he could acquire anything of monetary value for the club. By having ownership stake, he was able to project a positive public impression of the United Arab Emirates abroad and gain the respect and renown of the public.

Fast forward to October 2021 and the conclusion of the £300 million deal to acquire Newcastle United by a consortium, 80% financed by the Saudi Arabian Public Investment Fund (PIF). It's possible that this may be remembered as yet another significant turning moment in history. The fact that the PIF is richer than the combination of all other owners is not the key point here. It's not about wanting to watch better football; even the former owners from the '90s want the same thing. The $430 billion PIF's wealth ensures that the public will likely turn a blind eye if they choose to. Amnesty International UK Chief Executive Officer, Sacha Deshmukh, wrote a letter to Premier League Chief Executive Officer, Richard Masters, expressing his organization's concern. The organizations declared that the way the Premier League approved this deal raised serious concerns about the integrity of English football, the practice of sportswashing, and the correlation between human rights and sport.

The Saudi government's ownership of the PIF contributed to the deal's protracted development. This is why there were so many questions and challenges to this deal, some even demanding its cancellation. There are many well-publicized areas of questionable conduct by the Saudi's. The murder of Saudi journalist Jamal Khashoggi in a Turkish consulate has been attributed to this nation. A country where women's and LGBTQ+ people's rights are restricted, and where human rights abuses are widely reported.

There are allegations that the crisis in Yemen has been exacerbated by war crimes committed by the Saudi troops. With a charge sheet like this, you can see why some laundering of your reputation in the eyes of the world would be welcomed. But at the conclusion of the takeover, certainly none of Newcastle's "Toon Army" appeared to mind. This is a major improvement and a path to show dominance in the league. For years, the club was bouncing between the top flight and the Championship and was again in serious risk of relegation at takeover time. A wealthy owner would modify all that, so the supporters can't be held fully responsible.

It's not just that they have plans to outdo Real Madrid and the like in terms of football in the next few years—with showy, pricey signings and state-of-the-art sports complexes. Following the examples of Manchester City's owners, it appears that this new breed of sportswashing owner will bring much-needed investment to the North East and the Newcastle area. Many high-paying technical positions were established in Manchester's City complex, prompting politicians to visit the area to boast about the economic boost the Premier League had provided for the United Kingdom. Famous images of Chinese President Xi Jinping, former UK Prime Minister David Cameron, and former City player Sergio Agüero were taken, at an opening attended by George Osborne, among others. It's understandable that a fan could forget about Amnesty International's broader questions about the Newcastle takeover after seeing the country's shiny new stadiums and stores.

Additionally, the former owner, Mike Ashley, was not exactly admired by the Newcastle faithful. Fans despised him for not investing in the team and renaming the famous St. James Park stadium after his company and the stadium's main sponsor (Sports Direct). His terrible treatment of employees was exposed in a parliamentary committee report. The novel Saudi conglomerate may not be perfect, but then again, neither is any other billionaire owner. It's only natural for some people to be envious of your club's wealth, but it seems odd that rival fans would pretend to have such in-depth understanding of international politics unless they were actively working to sabotage your contract.

It is important to remember, however, that this Newcastle turning point occurred in the same year that the Premier League was feeling the pressure of the big clubs possibly breaking away to join the proposed European Super League. Eventually, this £300-million project was abandoned due to strong pressure from human rights activists and backlash from politicians and the public in general—removing the public approval these owners were seeking. Regardless, what is certain is that they have taken a huge leap away from football's working-class roots.

Mansour began his new business endeavor in 2013 when he established City Football Group (CFG), Manchester City's parent company that would go on to buy both majority and minority holdings in clubs throughout the world in an effort to expand their global reach. The entity Abu Dhabi United Group Investment & Development holds the main stake in CFG, 81% to be exact. The chairman of CFG and an Emirati government official, Khaldoon Al Mubarak, was accused of having given the green light for large sums of money to be transferred to the club's account. As a result, the club allegedly violated the financial fair play regulation on many occasions due to their excessive expenditures.

Even though they admitted guilt for violating UEFA regulations in 2014, by 2020, they had managed to have that finding overturned. These rules are meant to preserve some semblance of fair competition in the league by limiting the financial risk-taking of football teams. Reports indicate that between 2012 and 2022, Manchester City spent a whopping €1.7 billion on players, making them the most lavishly funded football team in the world. The fund has intimate ties to what Amnesty International considers "one of the most repressive police governments in the Middle East." In the United Arab Emirates, if you don't agree with the government, you'll go to prison. This is because the United Arab Emirates has the highest concentration of political prisoners in the world. According to Human Rights Watch, low-wage workers such as migrant babysitters or construction workers are being "forced to labor." But that didn't deter the Labour council members who were in charge.

For someone who was already one of the richest individuals in the world, purchasing a struggling soccer team in 2008 was a major step forward. To this end, his investment fund was now working with the British government, albeit on a limited scale, to acquire prime real estate and alter the city's skyline.

The collaboration's benefits to Sheikh Mansour were substantial. He was a member of the ruling family of a totalitarian state known for its brutality and dependence on oil revenues. Almost everything in Manchester, including public land in terms of hectares, zoning regulations, and government funding, was under the council's control. Nonetheless, data from Sheffield University suggested that Sheikh Mansour actually took home the bulk of the cash. According to Leaver et al (2023), nine locations were sold to Mansour at prices well below market value and below the sales prices of comparable properties in the area. The council claims it employed third-party experts and industry standards for values, but it won't elaborate. All of their leases were for a staggering 999 years. Additionally, the fund transferred property previously owned by the public to Jersey-based entities. Blocks of privately owned land by a member of the affluent elite, of a harsh dictatorship in an offshore tax haven, are now visible to pedestrians along the waterway between New Islington and Ancoats, and he didn't even pay a reasonable price.

This is the dismal verdict of the first comprehensive examination of the Manchester Life program, which was conducted after months of reviewing corporate records and planning applications. At times, the city council would prefer to attack its detractors than hear them out. After 25 years at the helm of Manchester City Council, in 2021, Sir Richard Leese stepped down. During his tenure, he had been very vocal about his disdain for those who advocate for more affordable housing.

Manchester is seen as a pioneer in a political landscape that is still finding its footing. George Osborne, the former chancellor of the Exchequer, has named its chief executive officer (CEO), Sir Howard Bernstein, the "star of British local government," and the Conservative government has lauded the Labour administration for its work. From 1997 until 2017, Bernstein presided over the council. Besides his work at Manchester Life, he was a member of the board there. The city may be prosperous, but its success has come at a steep cost to the city's population. The goods they possessed were sold at low prices, and they were given little in return. There are no low-income or social housing options on any of the nine constructed sites. The planning staff at the council gave reasons like, "There are already a lot of low-cost dwellings in the region," to justify this decision. Since 2018, the same council reported that approximately 4,000 resident youngsters, stayed in shelters on a nightly basis.

Apartments with two bedrooms in the Manchester Life buildings often sell for £369,000, which is considered criminal by most. A couple earning a middle-class income would struggle to afford this. Payments to the Exchequer look like a complete and utter farce. Over the five years prior to 2021, one of its primary companies earned over £26 million, but paid less than £10,000 in taxes. This equates to a tax rate of just 4 pence per £100 of income. However, it declined to disclose its annual revenue or the amount of taxes it pays. New Islington and Ancoats were not quite as nice as they are now, even five years ago. Who exactly has benefited from the shifts, and who has been harmed by them, is the million-dollar question. The fact that Manchester Life is a government-funded and -operated initiative makes it difficult to estimate its cost.

Most likely, Sheikh Mansour is aware of the exact amount of money he is making from Manchester Life, and he has hundreds of years of rental revenue from the land in this magnificent metropolis to look forward to. This arrangement appears to satisfy him. Mansour, who owns City Football Group, hired Bernstein as a senior strategic adviser shortly after he left the council.

Multisport Tournaments in Saudi Arabia

At first glance, the decision of Saudi Arabia's government to promote Western sports and entertainment may appear to be a major step forward in modernizing and progressing the country. After all, opening up the possibility for women to play in broadcast sporting competitions is a giant leap forward, especially in a monarchy where the interpretation of Islamic law was so stringent that women were not allowed to work in the public sector, go out in public without a male guardian, or even wear certain types of clothing without covering their hair and full body. This drastic shift caught the attention of many, both local citizens and members of the international community. However, it was also staged with great care, up to the point that it prompted discussion over whether or not Saudi Arabia is actually reforming or simply glossing over its serious human rights breaches.

Since 2016, sports have been a centerpiece for Crown Prince Mohammed bin Salman to achieve his vision for the 2030 Economic Development Initiative. Attracting foreign investment is not simply a matter of pride and a good image for this country, but also a strategic decision to expand their economic status by maximizing the potential of their large population, which is dominated by young people under the age of 30. To establish the framework, the government established preliminary discussions with various major American sports leagues in 2018, including Formula 1, Major League Soccer (MLS), the National Basketball Association (NBA), and the World Surf League (WSL), through their ambassador to the United States, Princess Reema Bandar al-Saud. The Saudi government spent over $650 million on infrastructure and training programs to bring these sports to the country and host these competitions.

The Saudis aren't the only ones who stand to gain from this ambition. For example, the partnership between World Wrestling Entertainment (WWE) and Saudi Arabia is mutually beneficial. For the Saudis, they have solutions for diversifying their economies away from oil—at least from what people see. For the WWE, this new investment will give them financial security after being hit by a scandal in which their former CEO, Vince McMahon, allegedly forced several women to keep quiet about his misconduct and inappropriate affair in exchange for monetary compensation. There are, alas, some stumbling blocks here. Western companies have been the target of boycotts in relation to the sportswashing charge because of the negative connotations associated with being seen to support a government with a longstanding history of oppression.

Given the timing of this trend—not too long after the murder of Jamal Khashoggi, a Saudi columnist for The Washington Post—it is hardly an exaggeration to suggest that all of this ambition is aimed at covering up the horrific human rights record and dodge responsibility after the Central Intelligence Agency conclusively proved that Prince Mohammed himself ordered the execution of Khashoggi. This can be seen in at least two occurrences; first, the decision of an electric motorsport race—the Formula E—to hold the season opener in Saudi Arabia just weeks after the assassination of Khashoggi. Second, Netflix removed an episode of Hasan Minhaj's show "Patriot Act" because it featured stand-up comedy that was critical of Prince Mohammed and the Saudi-led military intervention in Yemen.

LIV Golf Tour

Even though all of the Western sports projects have been widely criticized from the start, the LIV Golf Series debacle elicited the most widespread public outcry—especially for those deeply affected by the 9/11 tragedy. The Saudi sovereign wealth fund sees this competition as a chance to popularize golf and provide lucrative contracts to top players, both of which will ramp up their international reputations and alter the perceptions of Saudi Arabia and other Middle Eastern nations in the eyes of Westerners. This approach has been adopted by LIV Golf's organizers as they seek to challenge the PGA Tour's status as professional golf's pinnacle over the past century. In their inaugural season, the LIV Golf tournaments offered the largest prize pools in the sport; $25 million was up for grabs each season, with $20 million in the individual tournament and $5 million for the team tournament. In addition to any appearance-based fees or signing-on rewards, it was arranged that the champion at each round would receive $4 million, the runner-up $2 million, and the last-place competitor $120,000.

Compared to other sports branches that the Saudis have been eyeing, this investment in golf is seen as a way to appeal to a new subset of sports fans—those who are older, more privileged, and more affluent than their younger counterparts. This demographic includes former President Donald J. Trump. He has already spoken his mind about his disapproval of the Saudis, even going so far as to blame them for the terrorist attacks. However, two LIV Golf Series competitions took place at Trump-owned facilities in 2022: the opening season at the Trump National Golf Club in Bedminster, New Jersey in July, and the season-ending team championship at Miami's Trump National Doral in October.

The 9/11 Justice, an organization founded by the relatives of 9/11 victims with the goal of prosecuting Saudi Arabian government officials they accuse of aiding and abetting the terrorists, has harshly denounced this decision. They are furious that Trump, having previously agreed that the Saudi government was guilty, has now changed his tune to benefit financially from Saudi efforts to clean up the country's international image through sports. These people are making their case with the help of declassified FBI documents that they say prove a direct link between 12 Saudi government officials and the terrorists in the lead-up to the attacks.

Terrorism remains a concern, but the business potential, or "attention economy," of LIV has piqued the interest of many. The term attention economy lies in the idea that attention from the public crowd has financial value. Sports are highly desirable in the attention economy because they frequently attract a large, in-person crowd. Especially, since its nature depends on the novelty and the in-the-moment, it's easy to get people to pay attention. Saudi Arabia's Public Investment Fund (PIF) appears to aid LIV in taking advantage of these characteristics to avoid public scrutiny of their illicit activities. Business expenses and revenues, such as those from broadcast contracts, should be easier to reconcile as a result (like prize purses).

When compared to PGA tournaments, LIV ran much more quickly since golfers began their sets at multiple holes simultaneously. In place of the usual 72, there were only 54 holes to be played—representing the LIV in Roman numeral. To boost its entertainment value, they provided an audio-visual spectacle with depth and color that excelled the standard broadcast golf tournaments. Greg Norman, the CEO of the series, is said to have hired David Hill, a famous entertainment producer who helped change the way Formula 1 broadcasts were done, to try to get the younger generation interested in golf.

The conventional format of golf tournaments is notable for many reasons, but one of the most salient is that even though the best golfers tend to attract the most media attention, they do not always come out on top financially. At the halfway point of the event, competitors are eliminated from the main competition. To lose and not win anything, your score must be lower than this threshold. Some of the game's biggest names have been quoted as claiming that their salaries don't reflect their stature in the league. Payouts made by LIV to attract great golfers appear to be an attempt to equate monetary value with the value of media coverage.

Heavyweight Boxing

In June 2019, a Mexican-American named Andy Ruiz Jr. shocked the boxing world by defeating Anthony Joshua for the first time in his career through a seventh-round technical knockout at Madison Square Garden in New York City. Six months later, in a rematch called the "Clash on the Dunes", Joshua and Ruiz Jr. fought again in Diriyah, a small town to the northwest of the Saudi Arabian capital Riyadh. Joshua wanted to win back his WBA, WBO, and IBF titles and avenge his loss. The fight, however, has come under fire for being seen as supporting Saudi Arabia's "sportswashing" campaign.

Diriyah, the old royal palace of the Al Saud family and now a UN-ESCO World Heritage Site, hosted the event "Diriyah Season," which is being promoted as a "not-to-be-missed collection of international sporting events." This was the first ever heavyweight world title fight conducted in the Middle East, and it took place at the Diriyah Arena, which has a capacity of 15,000 audience and was created specifically for the occasion by UK exhibitor and developer *Arena*.

Nevertheless, skeptics maintained that the government sought to white-wash human rights abuses by using the fight and other sporting events like the Diriyah E-Prix, Diriyah Tennis Cup, and the Diriyah Equestrian Festival. A total of 146 beheadings took place in Saudi Arabia in 2019, with many of them occurring in Riyadh's Al-Safaa Square—in English, it means "Justice Square," often dubbed the Chop Chop Square—which is located only 10 kilometers (6 miles) to the south of the posh downtown hotels where Joshua and Ruiz Jr. would be staying.

Some human rights activists, such as Amnesty International, have urged Anthony Joshua to become familiar with the human rights situation in Saudi Arabia and be prepared to speak out; however, Joshua repeatedly dismissed this criticism, claiming instead that he was aware of the situation and working toward a relationship with the Saudi government. Even more forcefully, his promoter Eddie Hearn claimed that Saudi Arabia might soon eclipse the UK and even Las Vegas as the most prestigious site for boxing, arguing that it is his obligation to look after the best interests of his athletes. Also, he thought the world was already in a poor situation, so if people wanted to criticize Saudi Arabia, they might as well criticize everyone. A reported $50 million was made by Joshua from the bout.

Formula 1 in Bahrain

At the 2016 Bahrain Grand Prix in April, top Formula 1 driver Lewis Hamilton caused a stir by showing up in traditional Middle Eastern garb and tweeted his excitement and respect for Bahrain's culture. Later, however, Hamilton made a further declaration before the 2021 race in Bahrain by stating that he doesn't think tourists should visit these nations, have a good time while they're there, and then leave without considering the local situation.

After Russia was stripped of its Grand Prix race in response to President Vladimir Putin's invasion of Ukraine in 2022, activists in the Gulf region gained new confidence that they could use Formula 1 to exert political pressure on the governments of Bahrain and Saudi Arabia.

More than 20 international human rights organizations and labor unions, as well as around 60 members of the UK parliament, all urged Formula 1 to acknowledge the seriousness of human rights abuses in Bahrain in March 2021. In a letter to Mohammed Ben Sulayem, the newly elected president of the *Fédération Internationale de l'Automobile* (FIA), about 90 European parliamentarians voiced concerns that the FIA and F1 were deliberately aiding sportswashing in Gulf countries and setting a conspicuous double standard by criticizing the crisis in Ukraine while disregarding the acts of Gulf governments. Members of parliament from five countries (Germany, Italy, Ireland, France, and the United Kingdom) called for an end to the conflict in Yemen and drew attention to the brutality and persecution of Bahrain's pro-democracy activists, including Hassan Mushaima, Dr. Abduljalil AlSingace, and Sheikh Ali Salman.

The seven-time world champion Hamilton is held in high regard in the Jau prison in Bahrain, where a large number of the country's pro-democracy protesters are being imprisoned. Ali Alhajee, a convicted felon, wrote to express his gratitude for his attention to these instances, noting that it has altered inmates' perceptions of sports like boxing. According to Hamilton, he constantly gets letters from people in distress. He thinks governments and powerful people should bear the brunt of reform efforts. As a result, he realizes the significance of leveraging his platforms to ensure that genuine discussions are taking place regarding the situation there.

In response to the claims leveled against it, the Bahraini government has said that initiatives to isolate the kingdom in the Formula 1 calendar are ridiculous and completely invalidate the substantial successes and professionalism that the country has displayed. In a statement, a government spokesperson declared that Bahrain recognized and appreciated the potential of Formula 1 to shine a light on human rights issues everywhere it does business, adding that the country has been a model for human rights reform in the Gulf and that claiming otherwise is out of touch with the truth.

The statement also mentioned non-government organizations (NGOs) which sought to address human rights violations, such as the impartial Ombudsman, with Nawaf Mohamed Al-Moawdah now serving in the leadership position. In February 2012, King Hamad bin Isa al-Khalifa issued a proclamation establishing his office and stating that the ombudsman and his deputy will be selected with the Prime Minister's authorization and per the recommendation of the Ministry of the Interior.

It has been questioned by human rights organizations whether or not the Ombudsman's office is really independent. In 2019, the Americans for Democracy & Human Rights in Bahrain (ADHRB) warned that the agency was alarmingly incompetent, in addition to growing evidence that it was really complicit in human rights offenses and fostered Bahrain's impunity tradition. Constant violations of human rights are a topic of focus for other advocacy groups as well. According to Reporters Without Borders, Bahrain is renowned for imprisoning journalists, particularly photographers and videographers, due to the country's authoritarian leadership by the Khalifa royal family. Bahrain ranks 168 out of 180 nations on Reporters Without Borders' World Press Freedom Index. The U.S. Department of State has issued a statement on Bahrain's human rights record, citing torture and other forms of brutal, dehumanizing, or horrific treatment by security forces; severe confinement conditions (including a lack of medical attention); holdups without cause; limitations on the liberty to speak freely; major restrictions on the freedoms of worship and assembly; and other abuses and significant human rights issues.

Dr. Abduljalil AlSingace is a good example. He is a political prisoner, a well-known scholar, and a prominent human rights activist. He was wrongfully convicted and sentenced to life in prison in 2011. Since July 8, 2021, he has been on a hunger strike in protest of his unjust imprisonment.

His action is driven because his scholarly work was taken away from him after he spent four years in prison writing and studying it by hand. Authorities have arbitrarily stopped letting him have weekly video chats with his family, causing him to escalate his protest by refusing to take his IV as his health deteriorates. Bahrain continues to ignore Dr. AlSingace's modest demand for the return of his intellectual property and the international calls for his freedom and an end to this hunger strike. No, Dr AlSingace is not completely alone. For their roles in the pro-democracy uprising of 2011, nine additional prominent human rights and opposition activists remain behind bars.

Chapter 3

Why Sports Can't be Separated From Politics

M ixing sports and politics can easily irritate people. It's completely reasonable for sports fans to take pleasure in them for no other reason than to marvel at the incredible displays of human athleticism, sportsmanship, and eye-pleasing skills displayed in the sports arena. While there is a valid argument for keeping politics out of the sporting field, it does not mean that the two have no bearing on one another. Our responses to every moment surrounding sports—from the most joyous (such as celebrating victory) to the most reprehensible (such as when athletes are disqualified due to a doping scandal)—are influenced by the social and political climates in which we live. In this sense, sports can't be understood in isolation from the social contexts in which they were developed.

DAVID CARLTON

The Inextricable Link Between Sports and Politics

The Significance of Sports for a Nation

Understanding the relevance of sports in society can help us better grasp the significance of politics and sports. Sports can be used on a community scale as a barometer for how well people are getting along with one another, as a tool for eradicating barriers among people, promoting a healthy lifestyle, challenging prejudice and bias, and as a means of instilling ideals of shared values and tolerance. Some sports, typically those with strong cultural ties like Japanese martial arts and yoga, were created to promote spiritual growth and social order. Thus, sports are an essential part of people's social lives, with ties to people's minds, morals, and networks stretching across the cultural spectrum.

Once the bonds between members of a community have been established, the nature of sports can further function to build a sense of competition. Although, to some extent, this nature can increase tension and trigger friction between individuals who compete with each other. It's also a good way to nurture the values of fair play and cultivate a positive attitude, whether when losing or winning. When devising a strategy in the face of competition, team members will engage in creative problem-solving which adds depth to experience, sharpens mental faculties, improves concentration, and encourages teamwork.

All of these functions and values will extend beyond the local community. On a national level, sports function as more than just a game; they're useful as a means to foster a sense of nationalism, ideology, and prestige. It's not surprising that many countries, whether democratic or not, have attempted to improve their sporting prowess in some way. During an international level's tournament, being able to stand on the podium with their country's flag waving and the national anthem playing can reinforce those nationalism and prestige values. Furthermore, this moment can be used by the government—or sometimes the geopolitical blocks—to show dominance and other superiority traits. It's plausible that governments would like to demonstrate their economic strength by showing that they are able to provide athletes with appropriate incentives for medaling and training facilities that are on par with the best in the world.

There are many variables that affect a country's chance of winning a medal, and financial capacity is only one of them. However, regardless of the likelihood, the government still benefits from sending a team to compete in international sporting events. Sending delegates to these kinds of events, especially the Olympics, is widely recognized as a sign of independence and helps to build national identity, all of which are critical in helping smaller or newer countries receive recognition in the international community as independent nations on par with having a flag, national anthem, or currency.

While United Nations membership is often cited as the only means of fulfilling this role, an increasing number of nations are actually joining the IOC before gaining full membership in the UN. This is evident from a comparison of the two organizations' membership numbers: the IOC has 206 members, while the United Nations has just 193. For various reasons, including the One China Policy that prevents Hong Kong and Taiwan from joining the United Nations, as well as the vetoes cast by Russia and China against Kosovo's independence, there are a number of countries whose membership in the United Nations is contested. Therefore, some countries use their athletes' participation in sporting events as a stepping stone toward more worldwide recognition in the future.

Apart from playing a significant role in establishing national identity in the eyes of the global community, sports also act as "soft power" by challenging the social and political status quo as well as shaping a new narrative over social issues. This can be seen when prominent athletes use their platform to speak up for injustice or make certain gestures on the playing fields during tournaments. Furthermore, the way mass media incorporate social issues in their sports coverage—instead of discussing only about the statistics, technicalities, and any details happening on the field—can influence people's perspectives.

Can Sports Ever be Neutral?

There are typically two scenarios brought up when discussing the need for sports to remain impartial. The first is when athletes use their positions to bring attention to social issues, whether through actions on the field or overt declarations on social media. The second is the consideration of human rights records when making bid judgments involving nations with problematic records.

For instance, when Mesut Özil, an Arsenal player, spoke out in 2019 in support of Uyghur Muslims in China, the club issued a statement that seemed to imply they had always followed the policy of not getting involved in politics. Consequently, they were uninterested in taking a stand, as they believe the content released merely represents Özil's individual point of view. But when one of their players, Héctor Bellerín, posted his opinion during the 2019 UK General Election with the hashtag #FuckBoris in his personal Twitter account, Arsenal did not react in a similar vein like before.

Cynics would say this is because Özil's comments may cause Arsenal to lose all future partnerships with Chinese investors and may result in the permanent suspension of Premier League broadcast rights in China, which are worth over $700 million.

It's possible that some people will contend that professional athletes are not allowed to voice their political opinions, and that the sports field is not the appropriate setting for carrying out political activities. This can be seen in the case of Naomi Osaka, a prominent Japanese tennis athlete who uses her platform to support the Black Lives Matter movement. To those who disagree with Osaka, the common refrain is that athletes should not express their opinions and should solely focus on their sporting career. In fact, a popular tactic to suppress elite athletes who dare to exercise their right to free expression about matters close to their heart is to raise the argument "wrong location, wrong moment, wrong ways," which seems to respect but devalue the issues the players care about at the same time.

If we're talking about maintaining sports' neutrality, it's true that the sports themselves should never be used as a propaganda weapon. Nonetheless, even declaring neutrality is itself a political stance. Especially when the most famous sporting championships are given to politically contentious countries while simultaneously ignoring all rational objections. Any effort to stifle criticism, rather than address it head-on, does more than only go against the values of international sports organizations; it also undermines the system and prevents it from improving for the greater good.

It is never the correct time or place to protest, if we see this phenomenon from the point of view of public figures who voice their opinions publicly. The political objective of those who wish to prevent the conversation about societal issues from obtaining a bigger audience is served when people in the field that is meant to be "politically free" are denied their freedom to speak. Nonetheless, it's a complicated question to determine where the limits should be placed on activism throughout sporting activities. In terms of sports clubs, employment contracts put limits on what players can do for their respective teams. Commonly, the club's stated purpose will include a more or less informal limitation on such behavior. However, if a player's actions hinder the progress of the team in a game or jeopardize the club's financial stability, the organization may be forced to make them behave differently.

Regardless of the members' political leanings, the club must establish ground rules for conduct in the event that something goes wrong. If such regulations were put in place, however, they would still be subject to public scrutiny. The Olympic Charter or professional conduct guidelines, such as those that apply to American football professional players, are two examples of less legally binding ethical codes and rules that set the bounds for behavior in a sports setting.

Chapter 4

Cheating and Corruption in Sports

T he commercialization of sports—with the stakes higher than ever before in monetary values—appears to provide fertile ground for the development of unscrupulous practices. Sponsors and fans alike are interested in winning, but many couldn't care less about the means. As a result, if an athlete commits a serious wrongdoing, their supporters may only wish they wouldn't get caught. As evidence, consider the fervent fan base that continued to cheer for Lance Armstrong long after he was exposed as a doper. Nonetheless, there is a major factor in the proliferation of cheating and corruption in sports; the fact that individuals in positions of authority often opt to do nothing about it, owing to personal bias or financial gain. Since they have worked so hard to reach where they are, they would prefer not to discuss anything that may put them in danger of losing their position.

Match fixing, fraudulent betting, doping, and money laundering are just a few examples of the numerous forms of cheating that permeate the sports industry. Apart from the lack of credibility in the sports governing institutions themselves, the sophisticated operations of these offenses oftentimes become the reason why it's so hard to detect and thoroughly get rid of them. To some extent, when the government and officials of the tournament are involved, sportswashing can be a go-to technique to avoid accountability, diverting people's attention, as well as controlling the narrative circulated in mass media.

Doping Scandals

The usage of doping is contradictory to the spirit of sports because it allows athletes to cheat the system by going beyond what is possible for humans in terms of physical performance, offering an unfair advantage over their opponents. Although improving athletic performance can be done in multiple ways, including by taking dietary supplements, training in high-altitude areas, or loading up on carbohydrates, the substances that are listed under the World Anti-Doping Association (WADA) are mostly synthetic compounds; such as anabolic steroids, stimulants, diuretics, hormone modulators, and narcotics. The domino effect, in which one user's success encourages others to follow suit and utilize doping, is another serious drawback associated with this practice.

When participating in a sport, it's important to take a look at what is the best way to showcase and evaluate participants' skills and character traits. For those who disagree with anti-doping rules, the distinction between therapy and enhancement has been a central point of debate. Anti-doping policy is in a precarious position if we don't think there's a moral distinction between the two. The justification for outlawing steroids and growth hormone is shaky if athletes may easily alter the drug's dosage or mix it with another enhancing drug to switch its intended use from medicinal to enhancement without triggering a positive test result. Some people say that using steroids helps athletes recover from injuries after a particularly hard training session that damaged their muscles. However, it's hard to tell the difference between that and using steroids as stimulants to make athletes more alert and less fatigued, which gives them unfair advantages in competitions. The ambiguity of this problem makes it hard to figure out where to draw the line in many situations.

A second group of people who don't like this doping policy argue that certain procedures, like using anabolic steroids or growth hormone in regulated dosages, might be better regarded as therapies rather than enhancements to get better at sports and aren't a threat to the core principles of sports. However, there are some challenges associated with using therapeutic use exemptions (TUEs). Basically, rules concerning TUEs are established to protect athletes' rights to receive necessary medical care without facing potential penalties due to the use of a banned substance or procedure. Unfortunately, there are risks of abuse if a drug on the banned list was made available for medical reasons, and there would be even more problems if the drug that initially was used to treat illness ended up being used to improve performance. Therefore, WADA has pretty clearly covered this idea: the TUE should not be given if the athlete is likely to get a performance boost that goes beyond restoring normal function.

Both in therapy and sports, it's important to know how to take care of your own body, including when to relax and when to push yourself. More investigation into the questions of significance and value would always be beneficial. Athletes may just rise to the top of their sport due to a combination of natural skill and hard work. There's no reason that should diminish the stakes of the contest. Indeed, in many sports, athletes find enough purpose in merely challenging the best in their field.

Russia's Doping Scandals and Its Correlation With Sportswashing

When the first elements of a plot that culminated at the 2014 Sochi Olympics were made public, and when more recent discoveries of a failed Russian cover-up involving the manipulation of test results, WADA unanimously banned Russia from international competition for four years. According to the terms of the ban, clean Russian athletes could still compete in the Tokyo Olympics, the Beijing Winter Olympics, and other world championships, but they had to do so under a neutral flag (with the name Russian Olympic Committee, abbreviated as ROC) and without using any of Russia's symbols, flag, name, or anthem. This prohibition not only banned them from taking part, but also from hosting any international competitions.

The cheating scandal has plagued sports for years, and Russia has become an international outcast as a result. This is one of the most recent and harsh punishments related to the scandal. Hundreds of Russian competitors, some of whom may have been implicated in the doping or the cover-up, nonetheless participated in Tokyo, as they did at the 2018 Winter Olympics in South Korea, prompting criticism that the punishment was too lenient. This point was verified when Russian figure skating prodigy Kamila Valieva, then 15 years old, tested positive for a banned substance the day after helping ROC win the gold medal in the Olympic figure skating team event.

On the other hand, opponents of these critics focused on the consequences for innocent sportsmen and the broader implications of angering one of the world's leading sporting nations. Russia had promised to hand over test results from its Moscow facility to anti-doping authorities as part of the settlement of that case. Results were found to have been tampered with or removed from that database. The integrity of the data pertaining to as many as 145 individuals with potentially questionable drug backgrounds was compromised.

Russian officials denied any involvement in a systematic doping program among their athletes, despite overwhelming evidence to the contrary. There is an effort by the Kremlin to strengthen its grip on power through various means, including sporting successes and an aggressive foreign policy. So, their overarching goal of dominating global power is consistent with their desire to win as many medals as possible in any international-level sporting competition at all costs—including manipulating doping's test results.

Doping Restrictions Are Still Needed—Yet From Different Point of View

Doping restrictions may seem antiquated and unnecessarily stringent to some, but they are grounded in sound research and medical practice. The topic continues to generate an emotional reaction whenever there are high profile cases. Perhaps we should stop thinking of doping as inherently immoral and instead believe that the prohibition on doping is justifiable in the same way that the given rules and laws of any sport are. All sports have a purpose, reflected in the governing regulations. There should be systems in place to incentivize desirable behaviors, create a level playing field for competitors, generate excitement for the audience, and so on. Discarding restrictions would undoubtedly violate the essence and sense of fairness of the sport itself.

The fact that the International Olympic Committee (IOC) did not ban all Russian athletes in the wake of the country's doping issue can be interpreted as a step in this direction. It has delegated to individual sports governing organizations the authority to decide how to handle doping athletes within their own sports, rather than adopting a unified, homogenous stance on doping across all sports.

Illegal Betting Industry

In order to fully understand the scope of illegal betting, we must first consider three broad types of betting in sports:

- White market refers to betting businesses that hold valid licenses to do business in every jurisdiction in which they accept bets.

- The gray market consists of bookmakers who are licensed in at least one jurisdiction but operate in regions where their product is unlawful.

- Unregulated gambling sites that operate in multiple jurisdictions are a major part of the black market. This is a form of international crime syndicate.

When it comes to gambling, the gray and black markets are both illegal, but the rules for those who run businesses in the gray market are sometimes ambiguous. With the proliferation of online gambling sites that accept wagers from customers in several countries, it can be difficult to tell which ones are legitimate. Unless people look at it through the narrow lens of whether or not the operator is authorized in the jurisdiction of the point of transaction, there is no clear line defining where one ends and the other begins.

The popularity of betting on sports in countries with restricted legal gambling laws has led to an increase in illegal online betting over the past two decades, along with the rapid rise in internet usage and the internationalization of western sports audiences. Because of the widespread availability of internet access, gambling sites can now advertise their services to users in countries where it is strictly illegal to gamble. The operators will often take advantage of preexisting political or legal conditions to operate offshore internet gaming sites in jurisdictions where they are less likely to be detected.

The interfaces used in illicit gambling are generally hidden behind locked doors, and access is only granted once the customer has been thoroughly vetted by a human agent (instead of a bot chat or other A.I. tools). Some examples of illegal behavior in this industry are using online gambling to launder money, selling compromised accounts from sports and bookmaker companies, hacking well-known betting operators to get information about their competitors, and running illegal betting operations on their own. Another developing problem is the application of cryptocurrencies. They provide a safe and nearly untraceable option for overseas remittances. With this, illegal gambling can be pursued with less risk of being detected.

Even though it is common knowledge that betting with unregistered bookmakers is, at best, unethical, there are cases in which even betting with legal bookmakers can be considered criminal conduct. When gamblers have access to confidential data about the leagues or tournaments on which they are placing bets, this is a likely scenario to play out. After betting on a number of different 2019 NFL playoff games, defensive back Josh Shaw for the Arizona Cardinals ended up getting a suspension from his team and league. In spite of the fact that the investigation conducted by the NFL did not uncover any evidence that any internal information was used or that any game was tampered with in any way, he was still given a suspension from being an active player for the remainder of the 2020–2021 NFL season. Because he is a professional athlete in the NFL, his actions were interpreted as putting the other players in danger and damaging the reputation of the league among its supporters.

Match-fixing

The term "match fixing" refers to the practice of illegally influencing the outcome of sporting events. People do this for a variety of reasons, the most common of which is the desire to acquire an unfair financial advantage in gambling-related circumstances. The involvement of gamblers, athletes, match officials, and umpires is common, and has far-reaching consequences for the integrity of sports at every level. Some common infractions that are often referred to as match-fixing are:

- misconduct by athletes, such as intentionally poor play or a match withdrawal for fictitious grounds

- knowingly contacting or trying to persuade a sports official to change the result of a game

- taking measures to eliminate or dramatically change the role that chance plays in a match's outcome (or any other aspect of the match, such as the points spread or an in-match occurrence)

- an official in a sporting event making a mistake in his or her interpretation of the rules in order to alter the course of play, the use of certain pieces of equipment, or the outcome of the game as a whole

- intentionally or unintentionally distorting data to bolster a wager or place a wager on a game

While the gambling business is often at the center of match-fixing scandals, there are occasions when betting isn't the driving force. Match-fixing, when unrelated to gambling, typically occurs because of a desire to do one of the following:

- guarantee a certain position in the upper league standings

- ensure the ability to compete against teams from weaker brackets for the next round

- gain a competitive advantage in the future by finishing in last place at the end of the season and receiving the first pick of the best new players in a draft system

In order to achieve these desired outcomes, it is common practice to bribe match officials or the opposing team to allow for a loss or to play less aggressively in an effort to avoid a loss. Even though these examples clearly go against the sports ethic of trying to win, they are still about success, either a delayed success or a way to try to win by cheating. When sports organizations lack the regulatory competence to prevent external pressures, match-fixing cases can have devastating effects. Those that bet on the outcomes of a contest are the ones who orchestrate the match-fixing, whether they are legitimate bookmakers or criminals. Since the perpetrators' major goal is to make money off of the match's betting market, this situation is more troubling than similar ones in which the primary goal is to achieve ultimate success.

Thriving in the Betting Industry

Sports betting and the subsequent interest in influencing game outcomes have opened up a new market opportunity in which success, superiority, and effort are not the primary drivers of profit creation, but rather deliberate errors. When it comes to betting, the long odds are set on the underdog (the team that is not expected to win), while the short odds are placed on the top dog (the team that is expected to win). If the underdog succeeds in triumphing over the favorite, a jackpot is won. It's much simpler to make a mistake and intentionally lose a game than it is to play flawlessly and come out on top. Due to the confluence of these two factors, a new market has emerged where players can influence matches in order to earn quick cash by intentionally losing.

Furthermore, unlike other sorts of gambling with inanimate objects, such as playing poker cards or other games utilizing dice, sports are played by human beings who are aware that their matches are part of the gambling market. In light of this, every player in the league understands that their every move could result in monetary gain. One example is the rising practice of paying athletes to alter the outcome of sporting events so that money may be made from betting on them.

There is a certain type of betting that can foster the practice of match-fixing. If you're looking to make up for slimmer profit margins by charging higher odds, single bets (straight bets) on the result of an event are viewed as more appealing. The problem is that the greater the demand for a certain betting offering, the more predictable its outcomes are and the higher the chance for those outcomes to be rigged. There are many cases when, due to the simplicity and convenience of forecasting the outcome of a single wager, betting firms (both legal or illegal) tend to favor many bets across several events, hence increasing the danger of bankruptcy for betting firms. On the other hand, depending on the number of wagers involved, the cost of fixing the game in multiple bets could be high, and the return on investment could be low. At the end of the day, bookmarkers will ultimately rely on a single wager to win over and keep clients.

It might be argued that sports betting poses an insurmountable long-term threat to the incentive structure designed to keep athletes highly motivated to succeed in their respective games. Current trends show that the risks will increase as betting markets grow internationally, get more intense, and are mostly unregulated.

Still Growing, Despite the Punishments

The practice of rigging sports matches is developing. With the prolif-eration of digital technology, its proponents are broadening their focus to include a wider variety of sports and leagues. More than 1,100 sporting events may have been tainted by match-fixing since the pandemic began, as reported by Sportradar Integrity Services, a major global technology corporation that employs its betting surveillance system (the Universal Fraud Detection System, or UFDS) and has partnered with over 100 different sports organizations and leagues (Cascon, 2022). More specifically, these red flags were raised during the first nine months of 2021 in 12 different sports spanning 70 different nations.

Due to its popularity and the highest number of bets on sports, football is the most susceptible to match-fixing related to betting, with at least 700 tournaments in 2022. Europe is the region where this problem is most prevalent, with roughly 382 illicit games throughout 2021. In terms of value, a report from the International Betting Integrity Association and H2 Gambling Capital has predicted that approximately $25 million is lost annually in the global regulated gambling market due to match-fixing. When put in context with the over $70 billion that sports bookmakers made in 2020, the sum seems minuscule.

One of the many biggest match-fixing incidents in modern-day tournaments occurred during a qualifier match between South Africa and Senegal for the 2018 World Cup on November 12, 2016. Joseph Lamptey, a referee from Ghana, gave South Africa a penalty kick, which helped them win 2-1. The penalty itself was for a handball, although it could be seen clearly that the ball hit Senegal defender Kalidou Koulibaly on his leg. Shortly after that, several independent institutions, including the Global Lottery Monitoring System, Sportradar, Genius Sports, and Starlizard Sports Betting Consultancy, found irregular behaviors in the sports betting market. They eventually reported solid evidence that gamblers knew what the score would be ahead of time. The Court of Arbitration for Sport found

Lamptey guilty of two counts; unlawfully influencing match results and making pertinent bets successful, resulting in a lifetime ban from FIFA's judicial body.

Money Laundering

The term "money laundering" refers to the practice of making legitimate funds obtained through criminal means, such as those obtained through drug smuggling, corruption, or tax avoidance. The purpose of the money laundering process is to make it appear as though the funds didn't come from a criminal enterprise, so it wouldn't raise any red flags when purchases are made with this supposed dirty money. Since the funds aren't seen as derived from illegal activities, they can be utilized for anything without concern of legal repercussions.

While this type of corruption can occur in any professional sport, some sports, such as football, rugby, horse racing, cricket, ice hockey, motor racing, basketball, and volleyball, have a larger market for money laundering than others. A 2022 report from the United Nations Office on Drugs and Crime estimated that at least $140 billion was being laundered annually through football, primarily through the acquisition of sports clubs or leagues, the trading of players, the forging of ticket sales, and the exploitation of players' image rights.

As far as the global economy is concerned, money laundering leads to systemic problems in the sports industry. It's possible for criminals to make their funds appear to be genuine by paying above-market prices when acquiring or trading footballers. Another option is to buy struggling football teams that have inadequate leadership, a small fan base, or are about to go bankrupt. It's one thing if they're criminals who also aim to make these clubs function efficiently. Unfortunately, most of them are just about making sure the fans of those teams get what they want, which is to experience the thrill of seeing their squad prevail—regardless of their quality off the field. This isn't about overpaying for a star player with the hopes of flipping him for a great profit down the line. They are only interested in using sports as a means of laundering money and have no consideration for the impact this has on the clubs they acquire or even the integrity of tournaments themselves.

Long-term Impacts

Many people have discussed how money laundering damages the global economy and the global financial sector. It ranges from more unstable financial markets to more corrupt government officials, both of which will hurt the country's finances in the long run. But less research has been done on how money laundering can negatively impact the international sports industry—although it's just as damaging as it is in the government or any other political setting.

Sports, as a part of show business, have long stood as a level playing field in which economic status is not a predictor of future success. Athletes, especially those from lower-income families, who once saw sport as an escape from financial hardship, are increasingly likely to lose faith in the sports industry as a whole. Furthermore, due to the increasing prevalence of doping, a growing number of athletes are exchanging long-term health concerns for quick and untenable benefits in competition, as though they discard the traditional value that sees them as positive examples for their physique.

The laundering of illegal cash through sports clubs or the trading of athletes will, over the course of a longer period of time, have an effect on the distortion of supply and demand. This would have the effect of flooding the player transfer market with overpriced players who are not worth the amount of money they were purchased for. This is a practical implication of the situation. Because the abilities of athletes and the salary they receive are no longer comparable, it is difficult for teams to shell out the enormous amounts of money that are required to have competitive squads. A different possibility is that teams with subpar management would be monetarily rewarded for their efforts, and as a result, they would have no motivation to improve their management, operations, fan involvement, or performance in any manner. If players believe that their performance will not necessarily affect either their salary or the financial success of their club, they may be dissuaded from giving their best effort, which can be detrimental to the team's overall success. In the worst-case scenario, it's possible that some sports fans will become dissatisfied with the industry as a whole and lose interest in the sports tournaments as a result of their unmet expectations.

Another Entry Point for Sportswashing

Apart from apparent human rights abuses committed by the government or oligarchs with strong ties to the ruling government, cheating and other organized crimes can also serve as an entry point for sportswashing. As long as there is a need to restore a broken reputation, sports are often seen as the most effective means to achieve that.

For example, the misconduct of Daniel Joseph Kinahan, an alleged high-ranking member of the Kinahan Organized Crime Group (KOCG), often known as the Kinahan Cartel, a significant Irish transnational criminal syndicate, ranked among the most high-profile cases of how sportswashing and organized crime correlate to each other. The U.S. Department of the Treasury's Office of Foreign Assets Control (OFAC) imposed sanctions on the KOCG in April 2022, along with six other key members and several business associates, including Hoopoe Sports LLC, a sports management and consulting firm located in the United Arab Emirates (UAE)—the country where Kinahan resided and which has long been suspected as one of their main operational locations.

His reputation for his role in international money laundering operations and narcotics smuggling was masked by his engagement in combat sports like mixed martial arts and boxing. The fighters and trainers Kinahan advised were forced to defend him or at least disregard the claims made against him, despite his reputation as a helpful advisor. This word was generally adhered to, not because persons involved in combat sports were bad, but rather because they were afraid to speak publicly about the issue—let alone blowing the whistle to authorities—for fear of retribution or being banned from the industry entirely.

British Boxing Control could not prohibit or strip him of his management license because of his calculated and safe involvement in sports as an adviser rather than as the official manager. This occurs because unlike roles like fighters, coaches, promoters, and managers, being an adviser does not necessitate a license. Because of his success in brokering world title fights and negotiating massive TV deals with other promoters, Kinahan rose to prominence as one of the sport's most influential figures. Anybody who crossed him would have to deal with him eventually. Others have speculated that, armed with such influence, Kinahan could maintain control of boxing and carry on his illegal enterprise even if he were to go to jail. Notwithstanding this likelihood, many were delighted by the US government's offer of a $5 million reward for information pertaining to Daniel Kinahans' arrest and conviction.

In 2012, Kinahan also established a boxing management firm called MTK Global to help him better assert control and steer the narrative. Formerly known as MGM, the company formed alliances with top-tier boxers like Josh Taylor, Hughie Fury, Terry Flanagan, Rocky Fielding, Michael Conlan, Billy Joe Saunders, and Paddy Barnes. Athletes such as UFC fighter Darren Till and WBC heavyweight champion Tyson Fury, both signed to MTK Global, were also able to vouch for his sincerity, which bolstered his reputation as a sport contributor. In 2020, Till posted a statement defending his connection with Kinahan alongside a photo of the two of them on social media. Till defended himself by saying that they had been friends for a long time before he entered MTK Global. Fury exhibited the same denial by dodging questions on Kinahan's punishments. He denied any association with Kinahan and said that he was "only a boxer," avoiding questions about a photo that surfaced online depicting the two of them. As a result of the Kinahan's sanctions, MTK Global's leadership decided to shut down in April 2022.

While the Kinahan case shows that wealth and connections don't always guarantee success, the fact that sportswashing was indeed implemented by persons committing serious crimes indicates that significant reforms to the governance of sports are definitely needed to avoid another Kinahan from assuming such a dominant role in the industry.

Chapter 5

Do People Really Care?

T he mainstream media, social media, and other digital alternatives have provided extensive coverage of the controversies surrounding the 2022 Qatar World Cup, as well as the Olympics in China and Russia, so it doesn't take much work to learn about the dark side of these glamorous international events. Given how many people are still enthusiastic to enjoy the games, a thoughtful concern arises: Do people really care about all of the human rights issues involving their favorite sports?

The Emotional Relationship Between Sports Fans and the Teams They Root For

Following sports news isn't always about the glitz and glamor. Even the best moments can be clouded by the risk of a downturn due to factors such as a drop in performance, a loss of points, or a scandal on and off the field.

There is, however, no denying the enduring fervor of sports enthusiasts. A number of studies have shown that fans continue to invest time, money, and passion in their favorite teams.

The typical annual expenditure of a British football fan is £712 ($857), which includes spending on subscriptions, travel, and items related to the sport. In 2018, a dedicated Premier League fan spent a whopping $1,118. This was a lot more than what the Post Office predicted a fan would spend each year, which was $276. Similar results were found in a survey of 2,000 American football (NFL) fans, with 84% saying they would abandon everything to witness a match live—whether on screen or in person. They can travel an average of 476 kilometers (296 miles) to attend an away match and devote around 46 hours per month to discussing and thinking about their favorite clubs (Fothergill, 2022).

From the perspective of athletes, participating in sporting tournaments can elicit powerful emotional responses. The body goes through a series of changes once the stress hormone cortisol is released, including a faster heart rate and shallower breathing, as a way to better prepare themselves for the potential pressures they may face. Seeing a teammate win or celebrating one's own triumph has been connected to a rise in testosterone, and this effect is amplified when the team is at its home stadium. An increase in testosterone causes their brains to produce more of the feel-good chemical messenger, dopamine.

Interestingly, all of this euphoria isn't limited to athletes. Nearly identical physiological responses to those experienced by the athletes they support can also be experienced by the fans who root for them. Cortisol levels rise during key points in a game in response to what they perceive to be a threat to their social selves. This is especially likely for devoted supporters who base their sense of social selves on the fortunes of their national team, as is the case at nation-based championships like the World Cup. At critical moments in a tournament, for example, an increase in cortisol levels among supporters may be an adaptive response, as it would help them deal with their own negative emotions should their favorite team lose.

The release of cortisol to cope with stress isn't always associated with something positive since it can affect our immune system as well. Therefore, devoted fans who experience intense frustration or excitement need to be aware that chronically elevated cortisol levels can be harmful to their health.

Aside from the physiological effects, being a loyal sports fan also shapes the way they see themselves and their social relationships with fellow supporters. The social support we receive as sports fans boosts our sense of identity and overall health. There's no better way for fans to share in the excitement of a win than by doing so with other faithful, close friends, and loved ones. Once the sense of community is established, these psychological impacts could last for days after the joyous moments in the game have occurred. Interestingly, this social bond wouldn't fade just because the favored teams performed poorly. Indeed, the converse is true: supporters whose teams have had less success are more committed to one another than those whose teams have done better. Fans of lesser-known football teams are more likely to go to great lengths for their fellow supporters, including brawling with rival fans, making financial sacrifices, and even risking their own safety, all in the name of their team. Some of the benefits of joining such a group could be the friendships that are formed there.

Statistics Prove That People Care More About the Entertainment, Not the Important Issues Behind Them

Nearly 1.5 billion people tuned in to watch the 2022 World Cup final, which was for the first time, held in the winter months. Based on FIFA's statistics, the 2022 World Cup tournament was watched by around five billion people. The association claimed that this reflected the number of people that watched tournament coverage across several devices and platforms. That included the 5.95 billion social media engagements generated by the 93.6 million posts made during Qatar 2022. Over the course of the World Cup, posts across all platforms reached a total of 262 billion people. The governing body of Qatar 2022 has revealed record revenues of US$7.5 billion from the competition's four-year commercial cycle, considerably enhancing the tournament's ability to be successful from a financial standpoint (Jones, 2023).

After both the World Cups in Russia and Brazil, a similar pattern emerged. According to a FIFA estimate, 3.572 billion people throughout the world watched the 2018 World Cup in Russia, with 1.12 billion individuals watching the final match between France and Croatia on TV, away from home, or on digital media. Each of the 64 games was a global television event, with an average live audience of 191 million.

The high number of viewers has proven that the enthusiasm for football was more than enough to secure billions of dollars in profit, despite the fact that almost everybody knows the darker side surrounding these events.

The capacity of sports to elicit strong feelings in spectators is one factor that contributes to the formation of emotional bonds between fans and the teams or athletes they root for. Large sponsors and host countries can use the fact that fans will maintain their loyalty to their favored teams regardless of what happens in the lead-up to the competition to their advantage. This claim is backed up by the results of a study that was conducted in 2022. According to the study, sports fans do not care if the team has been accused of sportswashing or engaged in any other ethically problematic practices (Kim & Manoli, 2022). The explanation for this is that devoted supporters are less inclined to express unfavorable sentiments about their team when speaking with other people. It's a strategy for preserving the tremendous sense of community that comes with being a devoted fan. Despite the widespread criticism of the practice of sportswashing, it may not matter much to many of its supporters. And even if they do, many fans are willing to overlook the club's scandals in favor of protecting their own sense of team pride and camaraderie.

These startling conclusions can shed light on the future of sportswashing and provide context for the phenomenon as it exists today. Fans are a vital part of the sporting industry's economic ecosystem, as their recurrent spending on tickets and merchandise helps keep the industry afloat. And sports fans are also the most essential factor in sportswashing. Without loyal fans, there will be no distractions that can be used by people with bad reputations to dodge the criticisms from experts, activists, and journalists.

Does It Mean People Are Complicit?

Loyal fans and professional athletes cannot be directly held culpable for the wrongdoings of a sportswashing regime. Regular fans aren't responsible for the cruel labor system imposed on migrants or the execution of minority groups committed by the host of any sporting event. Most of the time, they are not even deeply embedded enough in any political ideology to be accused of supporting tyrants who violate basic human rights. However, this does not rule out the possibility that one's complacency as a fan has contributed to the escalation of human rights violation instances.

Sportswashing is used to cover up human rights violations—if the world tried to put pressure on these regimes, the focus for these issues would be maintained and less distraction of sporting events. Therefore, anybody involved in sports (including league executives, athletes, and fans) can be deemed complicit in these injustices by facilitating the practice of sportswashing, which permits these injustices to persist.

This scenario played out when the manager of Newcastle United, Eddie Howe, was questioned about his thoughts on Saudi Arabia, Newcastle's new majority shareholder, with regard to the deaths of 81 innocent individuals in that country. When pressed and asked if he would go on record condemning the actions, he demurred, insisting he would only speak on football matters. This behavior is not limited to Howe; other public figures engage in it as well. Managers and players for sportswashed teams often stay silent about the wrongdoings of their owners.

Because of its politically loaded message, this remark is extremely troubling. By making it clear that the sports teams themselves have no correlation with the actions of their owners, fans are more likely to be lenient when the clubs' new business leaders benefit from the positive publicity. Loyal supporters are reluctant to criticize their teams; therefore, they attempt to separate the teams from the wrongdoings of the owners while still providing credit to the owners. The same holds true for players who choose to remain silent despite having knowledge of misconduct on the part of their coach, general manager, or owner. In the end, sportswashing is a process that involves more than just the government. It involves both fans, management, and athletes. Since sportswashing could end up hiding an injustice, those who do it could result in making that injustice worse as well.

So, how about those ordinary people who find enjoyment in watching sports games; can they be complicit just because they *choose* not to care about politics or issues that don't affect them personally?

There are generally two distinct types of sports spectators: those who remain silent and those who defend or justify those who violate the rights of others for the sake of their favorite team. It may sound insensitive, but those who are friendly toward abusers are sometimes protected by the sports community as one of their own, especially when facing criticism from others who are not part of the group.

This is especially true when the criticism is coming from outsiders. This was made very clear when fans of Chelsea Football Club shouted the name of their Russian tycoon patron, Roman Abramovich, in the middle of a round of applause during the match as a show of support for Ukraine. Because of Abramovich's close relationship with Vladimir Putin, the actions of Chelsea supporters could be interpreted as a way to undermine the effectiveness of sanctions imposed on the Russian government. It would appear that sportswashing lowers the morality of fans because it makes unethical behavior seem more commonplace and tricks them into accepting things they ought to despise.

Those who choose to stay silent while still enjoying the hype of the events are still rendered complicit under two circumstances. First, financial benefits. Sportswashers not only put a lot of money into it, but they also profit from it. If a fan wants to see a game, they must either pay for entrance to the stadium or tune in to watch it on television. The sales of tickets, broadcasting rights, advertisements, and merchandise all bring in cash for the sportswashers. Eventually, this sum of money ensures the sustainability of sportswashing.

Second, emotional attachment. The support of the fans is crucial in making a team or tournament successful. One reason the World Cup is so significant is that it captures the interest of people all across the world. Sportswashing can also rely on the reputation and prestige of the events themselves rather than monetary incentives alone. Sportswashers are aware that there is always a certain vibe at sporting events due to the passion of the supporters. This positive association is what makes sportswashing possible in the first place. All spectators are indirectly in on the crime if they join in the jubilation following their team's goals and other customary fan behaviors.

Most sports leagues and clubs have been around for quite some time, and their histories are often storied and celebrated as the very fabric of local culture and a key component of local pride. It is the strong ties to the local community that give this way of thinking its foundation, not the success or prosperity that have resulted from it. One of England's biggest clubs, Newcastle United, is an example. They haven't won a major trophy in decades, yet they can still draw a devoted fan base in their home town. Many people, from regular citizens to professional athletes and officials, place a high value on these activities because of their long history and strong sense of community. Most of these clubs are now just big businesses, so all of the original lofty goals have been turned into something that can be used to fix an owner's bad reputation. With the support of fans who don't care about their owners' unlawful track record, the sportswashers utilize the club and their devotion for their own ends.

The strong ties to the community mean that fans of a particular team might remain devoted for decades, if not generations. Many factors may come into play during this time, including the fan base's expectations for the team's style of play, the club's commitment to the local community, and the club's ability to attract and retain players who embody the ideals of the organization. Undoubtedly, though, triumphs are the most potent motivator for followers to remain loyal. It's no surprise that these supporters want the club to succeed given how much it means to them. The sportswasher makes frequent use of this fact, at least when it comes to the ownership of a club. In any case, when the team is successful, the sportswasher will be held in high esteem, and the supporters will defend him or her just as they would a beloved coach or player.

Aside from the positive way these deeply emotional ties can bring people together, there are two ethical issues that are unfortunate. Firstly, sportswashing has the potential to make viewers solely focus on winning, rather than on the broader social and cultural values that are fostered through sports. This has the potential to devalue the experience of being a fan by substituting the deep bonds shared by the community with a shallow desire for winning. Rather than being exclusive to sportswashing, this issue is typical of the commercialization of sports in general. The second is how sportswashing may dry up the shared values of morality and ethics. This can be demonstrated when fans either openly defend or deny that their favorite sports team is associated with morally questionable regimes.

The ability to just enjoy the spectacle of the tournament may also be compromised for supporters who follow for the love of the game but have no allegiance to any one club. Unfortunately, they have to watch while those with poor records reap the benefits of the tournament's hype and financial windfall. The basic joy of witnessing that sporting event is gone for many spectators, as soon as they know the horror of human rights abuses. This does not diminish just because the tournament is successfully held. If the competition is tainted, the fans' experience of the event will be tainted as well. While we have been looking at the cultural values that are linked with sports, this example shows that even the more archetypal sporting ideals—the idea of effort, fairness, and natural athletic potential—may be compromised. The impressiveness of these remains intact, but they have been compromised by being put to use in a fraudulent effort to clean soiled names.

How People's Ignorance Shapes the Way Sports Teams React to Social Issues

The chance to prevent those committing human rights violations from enjoying impunity is hampered when fans don't care about the social issues at the heart of the sportswashing allegations. Due to this ignorance, the value of sports institutions aren't automatically boosted only because people see them as socially responsible entities. This situation will remove any incentive for sports organizations to alter their procedures and become more proactive in addressing societal problems. In light of this, it would appear that sports clubs are not given much—if any—motivation to uphold the moral standards in their commercial practices. Many of their fans will likely remain devoted even if they face criticism from activists and the public at large.

Chapter 6

Sports Sponsorship: When "Greenwashing" Becomes Common Practice

G reenwashing has long been a go-to strategy for businesses look-ing to hide their negative effects on the environment. The phrase "greenwashing" itself refers to advertising campaigns that falsely claim a company's products are environmentally friendly when they are not. One can accomplish this in a variety of ways. Car companies, fcr example, often claim that their newest models have low emissions and are good for the environment, but some have been proven to cheat on the emissions tests. Similarly, in an effort to reduce their environmental impact, fast food restaurants have publicized their switch to a new lid that seemingly doesn't use plastic as its main material, despite the fact that it produces more emissions than the previous plastic straws they also replaced with paper straws.

This practice has become more widespread as concern for the environment has grown. In order to convince consumers that purchasing their goods will make them heroes, some companies use narratives about their significant contribution to nature without giving any details on how to verify those stories. This can allow companies to convince consumers to buy products they otherwise wouldn't. Fortunately, educated and environmentally conscious individuals who are curious about the processes involved in product creation and the effects on the natural world wouldn't easily fall for companies' empty claims. Moreover, these companies are more likely to make active contributions to environmental organizations, through donations or volunteering.

Greenwashing typically occurs when a company engages in any of the following three practices: employing ambiguous or deceptive language in their marketing; failing to back up or verify environmental claims; or concealing facts regarding the environmental impact of their production process. In most cases, companies that portray their activities in this way fail to factor in a very important aspect of business: production and supply chain emissions. This includes the carbon emitted in the manufacture of the materials and the diesel burned by the trucks, trains, and sea vessels that ship these materials to and from factories and onward to buyers' homes.

In addition, once the aspects of a product's lifespan are considered, many claims to eco-friendliness and carbon neutrality fall flat.

Since concern about the impacts of climate change on human health and the environment is growing, sports fans are increasingly likely to question sponsorship arrangements with corporations that have morally questionable practices in terms of sustainability.

Greenwashing in Sports

In addition to endangering human and environmental health, climate change poses a threat to the development of sports in the years to come. It may be difficult to hold well-known outdoor sporting events if temperatures reach 50°C degrees Celsius by 2040. But the climate problem is already having an impact on major sporting events. The 2019 Rugby World Cup was interrupted by a typhoon, while the Australian Open was canceled due to the toxic smoke from the country's horrific bushfires. Some experts predict that in the next 30 years, it will be more difficult to host the Winter Olympics due to rising temperatures, and that a quarter of English football league fields will be at risk of flooding every season due to rising sea levels.

Since many big corporations are heavily contributing to this climate catastrophe and involved in major sports sponsorship, it's very likely for sports to also be used for greenwashing. But the sports themselves need to make their own changes to prove they're on the winning side of the climate crisis fight, whether it's converting from aircraft to trains for travel, eliminating single-use plastic in stadiums, or cutting ties with fossil fuel companies. Greenwashing and sportswashing often occur concurrently, but not necessarily. The strategies FIFA had in place to offset carbon emissions for the 2014 and 2018 World Cups, for instance, were heavily criticized by environmentalists. The goal of these initiatives was to mitigate the environmental impact of international travel by football fans to the stadiums where the matches were held.

When companies who have negative track records in terms of environment begin to support sports in any way, fans or the public in general will eventually begin to link the brand's logo and name to their most cherished sporting moments. This seems like a direct support for those companies willing to invest higher. Positive emotional associations with a brand will push their products to the forefront of the mind over competitors who don't invest in sports, increasing the likelihood that consumers will continue to use that brand. These heartfelt linkages can divert our attention from the negative role that businesses play in pollution and global warming.

However, from the perspective of sports clubs that accept funding from dirty energy sources like coal, gas, and oil, their long-term image and credibility may be damaged. Over time, growing public concern about the potential negative effects of corporate sponsorship on individual and community health has forced sports leagues to shift away from accepting funding from morally questionable sources. There have already been laws passed that make it harder for businesses like tobacco, alcohol, and gambling to use sports as a form of advertising. Maybe these energy sources will follow.

The United Nations held a workshop in Bonn, Germany, for two days in October 2017 to bring together experts in the fields of sports and environmental research. The event planners reached out to sports organizations like FIFA, UEFA, and the Philadelphia Eagles from the NFL to see if they could spread the word to their followers about the urgency of addressing climate change. These discussions resulted in the United Nations'

Sports for Climate Action Framework. Intentionally vague objectives were presented alongside the initiative's debut at the United Nations climate summit a year later in 2018. The framework required its signatories to commit to high-level goals, such as a cut in carbon emissions. Signatories were also instructed to make sure the participants were willing to measure greenhouse gas emissions to establish a baseline impact.

Teams and leagues were quick to sign this framework: organizations including the IOC, the New York Yankees (MLB), the Golden State Warriors (NBA), and Liverpool FC (EPL), as well as local initiatives like the Grandma's Marathon in Duluth, Minnesota, and the Austrian Ocean Race Project. In light of the positive attention they received, many of those who signed the declaration were keen to elaborate on their interests about the initiative. Unfortunately, only a small percentage of those participants followed through with their promises. One year after the framework was established, in 2019, the UNFCCC requested information on whether or not its signatories were tracking their greenhouse gas output. There were 249 signees at the time, with more than 60% of participants having not even begun to measure.

Many sports organizations supported the UN's accountability system and were correct to call for the measures. For instance, the IOC boasted in news releases leading up to the 2008 Winter Games in Beijing that all of the city's venues would be run on green energy. However, years later, they never mentioned that Beijing 2022 destroyed a mountainous nature reserve to make room for several facilities, or that they diverted groundwater to make the 1.2 million cubic meters of synthetic snow that coated every ski slope.

The most common way that people try to give the impression that they are environmentally conscious without actually being so is through the purchase of carbon offsets. It attracts teams and other clients with its low prices and positive publicity, but it is unclear how the profits from selling carbon offsets are used to protect the environment. One of the most popular methods of creating offsets is planting new trees. The Birmingham 2022 Commonwealth Games claimed to create a legacy in terms of environmental preservation. In order to ensure carbon neutrality, the committee planted 2,022 acres of forest in the Midlands through a partnership with a third party. While planting trees can help mitigate climate change in the long run, it won't help with emissions reductions in the short term because it takes decades for a tree to reach maturity and begin eliminating carbon from the oxygen we breathe.

Miscalculation of carbon emissions and misleading interpretation of carbon offsets are not the only issues to be concerned about. The cryptocurrency market and industrial carbon footprint both have negative environmental impacts and significant links to the sports business. Bitcoin's annual electricity use is roughly 97.93 terawatt hours, which is more than the annual consumption of the entire country of Belgium. Multimillion dollar crypto investments have been made in several major sports, including e-sports, Formula 1, the UFC, and Manchester United FC, in an attempt to develop relationships with sports fans and maintain a good reputation. It is predicted that by 2026, this rapid growth will have reached $5 billion.

Some crypto companies, such as Bitcoin, Shiba Inu coins, Tezos, and Dogecoin, have come to realize that engaging with wider communities is essential to the success of their products, whether it's for marketing, funding, or driving up the value of the underlying coin or token. Some cryptocurrency firms provide "fan tokens," which are essentially cryptocurrency products that are tied to a specific sports team or league and can be used to show support for that team by, for example, purchasing tickets, providing special offers on merchandise, forming a fan community, and casting votes on matters pertaining to that team. This is a great strategy for reaching the same young people that traditional brands like Coca-Cola and Heineken have been advertising to for years. Thus, these businesses have increased their brand recognition among sports fans.

Big Money is Involved

Corporate sponsors from the fossil fuel and mining industries frequently use sports team sponsorships to improve their public image. As more people become aware of these corporations' roles as major contributors to the greenhouse gasses that cause climate change, they become increasingly concerned about losing public trust in their brands. They've spent millions on PR to frame themselves as "the good person" in the fight against climate change. To divert this wide criticism, they provide financial support to sports organizations on a global and national scale, capitalizing on the positive image sports enjoys and the devotion of its supporters.

In 2022, a report from Swinburne University of Technology determined that fossil fuels companies spent about $14-18 million a year to sponsor sports in Australia. It's true that this figure isn't exactly negligible, but it may be adjusted in the years to come to make it less conspicuous. The name of the sponsor is often prominently displayed on team jerseys and at stadiums as part of the lucrative naming rights deals that are commonplace in these industries.

Santos, an oil and gas firm based in South Australia, is one of the most philanthropic companies in the world, having donated to a variety of different sporting organizations. Prior to adding the Wallabies to its long association with Rugby Australia, Santos sponsored the Wallaroos, New South Wales Waratahs, Western Force, Queensland Reds, and the Australian Women's Sevens. Aside from funding the top athletes and teams, Santos also sponsored the Aboriginal Power Cup in early 2021, a football competition for Indigenous high school students in South Australia, in conjunction with the Port Adelaide football club, and the Festival of Rugby in Narrabri, where the rock band Thirsty Merc served as the headlining act.

Santos was also the "official gas partner" of the 2021 Australian Open and sponsored the Tour Down Under. However, Tennis Australia's website does not feature the company's logo. This sponsorship deal was met with criticism. The tennis association was accused of sportswashing since it was perceived as giving Santos a stage to promote the use of fossil fuels as though it had no significant environmental impact. Tennis was one of many sports that suffered greatly as a result of the climate crisis. A real example of how far the climate crisis affects sports can be seen at the 2014 Australian Open. A game was suspended, and 1,000 fans got medical treatment for heat exhaustion after temperatures reached more than 40°C. After a petition signed by over 7,000 individuals was delivered to Australian Open CEO Craig Tiley, and approximately 300 athletes campaigned for sports bodies to take more concrete action on tackling the climate crisis, the agreement was terminated at the end of 2022.

When polluting companies pay for sports events, it sends the message that this kind of behavior is acceptable and has no contribution to combating the climate situation. If in the past the sports industry has rejected tobacco sponsors, it should apply the same standard by turning down the dirty money offered by the coal, oil, and gas industries.

Sports Fans Reactions to These Sponsorship Issues

Since the world's sports industry produces as much carbon dioxide as a small country, it stands to reason that sports governing bodies and prominent athletes should play a significant part in combating climate change. The owners of sports clubs and the organizers of sporting events have become the primary targets of fan protests during the past several years. Because activism has a significant impact on profitability and stock prices, negative headlines might cause the company's "goodwill" in sponsorship to turn against it, further tarnishing the company's reputation.

Since greenwashing is a deceptive marketing strategy that aims to increase demand for environmentally friendly items, many consumers may have no idea if the decision they're about to make in terms of which products should be bought or not is the right one. Consumers' risk aversion and subsequent behavior in the face of greenwashing may be directly related to the degree to which they believe the marketing claims made by the company. Companies that engage in greenwashing risk having their customers distrust them and reduce their likelihood of future purchases as a result.

Many studies have shown that consumer confidence in a company decreases when they suspect that it is engaging in greenwashing. Therefore, research is crucial for businesses, markets, and governments because it provides insight into consumer behavior and mindset. It's an essential aspect of scientific inquiry into how to make the economy and society as a whole more resilient in the long run. Most people don't like taking chances, so it's crucial to understand how greenwashing influences consumers' risk aversion when making purchases. Most of the time, the mere mention of risk causes people to feel uneasy and motivates them to seek out other alternatives that are seen as more responsible. A consumer's awareness of greenwashing influences not just their impressions of a company's products but also their feelings about the company as a whole and their willingness to buy their products.

While we can rely on environmentally conscious fans to make wise purchasing decisions toward companies committed to greenwashing in sports, the fact that there are still a significant number of fans who may not put environment as an important consideration before purchasing something may have important implications on the practice. The strong emotional bonds in sports makes it easy for fans to see the similar values between sponsor companies and sponsored teams. Especially, if the companies make campaigns dedicated to the teams or events rather than just putting the logo and brand's name in the stadium or jerseys. Fans may see it as a strong message on how the companies promote the same values as the teams, making them perceived as socially responsible institutions that strive for natural preservation and healthy lifestyle. These perceptions could elevate the worth of the goods in fans' minds by adding to the intense joy around the sports teams or events. The more valuable the greenwashers' products are, the more likely the fans are to prefer them over those of the competition.

From the standpoint of sports fans, there are robust relationships between how they feel about a given brand's sponsorship of a certain sport and the likelihood that they will patronize that brand. In addition to the emotional ties that form between fans and their favorite teams, the beneficial impact is also due to the words and values promoted by firms through sponsorship. This correlation occurs because fans are more likely to pay attention to sponsors whose messages amplify their own personal beliefs while also reflecting those of the group to which they belong.

Chapter 7

Why It Matters: How Sportswashing Will Negatively Impact the Democracy

I t's easy to sideline anything about sports when discussing democracy because most people would see those as two separate entities with no correlation at all. Unfortunately, any scandals and violations of the law can influence and be influenced by the democratic dynamics of the given country.

In the context of democracy, there are three essential paradigms: by the people, for the people, and of the people. These principles ensure everyone, both ordinary citizens and the authorities, have equal rights in expressing their opinions, contributing to decisions related to passing laws and regulations, and choosing or being chosen as candidates that are deemed suitable to sit in governing bodies.

These three tenets are grounded in a larger ideal: the belief that every person should be treated with the utmost respect and decency. Only by granting liberty and equality can this value be safeguarded. People's rights are not decided by the privilege of their ascendant; therefore, these fundamental values form the basis of modern democratic-liberal societies, whose primary goal is to make human beings thrive and prosper. In spite of its progress, modernism is still a work in progress since these objectives are so far from being realized. The foundation of our society is the promotion of more equitable and freer individual members, and this principle should also guide the development of modern sports.

The democratic aspect of sports extends beyond the administrative level, in which there could be formal autonomy and decision-making mechanisms, but it lies in the practical level as well. This occurs because democracy is about much more than simply rhetoric and votes. The right to free speech is central to the democratic ideal, and sports provide a highly visible arena in which this principle can be exercised. When it comes to expressing an individual's views, sports can be a "safe area" for everyone, from elite performers to regular individuals. Sports teams with broad and inclusive fan representation can better reflect the voice of the people due to strong emotional ties and fewer barriers among fellow supporters. This aspect, in conjunction with other strategies, could improve the application of democratic principles generally or sports policy in particular.

Sports and the Value of Democracy

Because of the rules and current dynamics that govern modern sports, they serve as a great example of how a democratic society should be run. In sports, neither privilege nor injustice can influence who will be the victor. The winners are decided on the basis of their merit—or, in this case, their athletic abilities and efforts. And the most important thing is that these achievements are not meant to last forever. This is why ancient Greek athletes were awarded crowns made of olive leaves: they represented the fleeting nature of victory and served as a reminder of the sport's transience. The ranks were constantly being replaced and renewed. Those who currently hold a championship or trophy should make more efforts to maintain them.

Unfairness does not necessarily arise from the fact that inequality exists. It is unjustifiable when this state of the situation is predicated on benefits and privileges that were unfairly obtained. Of all, this sort of unfairness goes against the whole nature of sports. As we've already established, sports should operate on a fundamentally level playing field. This is why strict rules related to doping, betting, and match-fixing are strictly prohibited because they hinder athletes and executives from upholding fair play. Consequently, sports have the potential to be used as a means of making our societies more equal, as this kind of sporting fairness is a drive that can influence the essence of the ideals of our democracy.

As we discover this driving force in sports, we come to understand that fairness will not be humbly bestowed upon us. But we need to figure out how to harness the power of sports and use them to our advantage. As a result, sports serve as a model of a free society due to the widespread acceptance of the principle that athletes have no inherent rights to anything inside the realm of athletic competition. In such a society, everyone would be on an equal footing, and those who could best demonstrate their superiority over others would take charge. Sports serve as a great teacher in this regard. As a result, we can conclude that sports play a significant role in the political and social fabric of our society. It has several beneficial qualities that make it a terrific method for improving our society.

Sports can be a powerful tool for people who want to change policy or society—a fundamental part that can only be done in a democratic environment. The United Nations and other international development organizations have used sports programs to advance gender equality, combat prejudice, and foster a culture of peace for the past two decades. President Nelson Mandela's support of the South African rugby team in 1995 during the World Cup, when the team represented the recently deposed apartheid state, is widely seen as a shining example of the power of sport in national reconciliation efforts.

There is little doubt that the IOC and FIFA can use their influence and high-profile events to advance human rights. The IOC's 2015 decision to develop a refugee Olympic team was a huge win for the cause of refugees and the difficulties they face. Overall, though, the results of these efforts have been mixed, and FIFA's recent claims that the World Cup spotlight has led to welfare and labor reforms in Qatar have been shown to be greatly exaggerated.

Does Sportswashing Damage Democracy?

The topic of how the practice of sportswashing can diminish the worth of democracy has grown in recent years as the media, the fourth pillar of democracy, has come under increasing attack for its unwillingness to tell objective perspectives in relation to sporting events or sports teams that have associations with sportswashers.

FOX is one of the most well-known Western media outlets that declined to discuss the contentious exploitation of migrant laborers in Qatar during World Cup coverage. When asked about this choice, David Neal, the executive producer of FOX's World Cup coverage, responded only that the network would only report events that had an impact on the game itself. He did, however, assume that other organizations and media sources would cover stories that didn't have an immediate impact on the tournament, including all of the human rights abuse allegations. He was adamant that viewers of the World Cup coverage would do so solely for the purpose of seeing what occurred on the playing field.

This is not the first time this has happened; at the 2018 World Cup, they also ignored condemnation of the Russian government. However, there was something different this time. FOX's broadcast in Qatar was practically being sponsored by the Qatari government, which has been widely speculated to be the reason for the decision as Qatar Airways becomes a key sponsor of the network's coverage. Neal first claimed in his remark to the Sports Business Journal that FOX would dispatch at least 150 employees and broadcasters to Qatar. Since the stadiums are so close together, the media company would become the first American broadcaster to have commentators present for all World Cup games. However, others familiar with the conglomerate's plans claimed that the network originally intended to conduct the vast majority of its operations from afar, sending only a select group of staff to Qatar. Those who spoke anonymously to discuss internal matters claimed that the strategy shifted only after the agreement with Qatar Airways was sealed. It was in 2021 when the airline and the news company began cooperating. Signs promoting Qatar Airways, the Gold Cup's principal sponsor, and FOX's coverage of the tournament were prominently displayed in the studio during the network's broadcast.

Many who believe that Qatari authorities should be held accountable for their misdeeds feel that FOX's decision to ignore the shady side of the World Cup goes against the ethos of journalism as a watchdog to acquire information about the behaviors of individuals in power and reveal that to the public.

When the public's attention can be successfully diverted from the misconduct into the enjoyment of sports games, it can give a sportswasher the confidence to commit even more crimes and contribute to the perpetuation of poor leadership. Of course, as the World Cup in Qatar demonstrated, high-profile sportswashing frequently received a significant amount of critical attention, raising legitimate concerns about the extent to which it poses a threat. Historical evidence suggests that negative reactions to a sporting event tend to fade once play begins, and the early indications post-tournament are that the 2022 World Cup in Qatar will be no different. Additionally, criticism does not necessarily imply that sportswashing is not effective. After all, the goal of those who engage in sportswashing is to enhance their reputations in general. One of the speeches given by FIFA President Gianni Infantino, in which he blasted Qatar's critics and dismissed human rights concerns, is a prime example of how influential voices inside sports governing bodies may help countries like Qatar achieve this goal.

Does It Work?

Despite all the effort to silence critics and divert people's attention, campaigns and reports in the media still exist—almost at a level where those with a tainted reputation can't interfere or make them disappear completely. For some, this constant pressure can be a hopeful step toward continuing the fight over human rights issues in the long term.

This does not mean, however, that the war against authoritarian countries hosting big athletic events is over. After all, we entered the World Cup with the knowledge that many large-scale sporting events have been organized in nations where citizens face oppression. But there is pushback: from fans in the comfort of their homes, from contrarian voices within Qatar, and from certain media outlets that don't get dictated to by big corporations. Even though it's still far from enough, at least the people who died and the communities that were hurt in the lead-up to this World Cup were remembered, chronicled, and advocated for in some ways.

There is potential for positive outcomes to result from anti-sportswashing campaigns. Though those in authority may use sports to cover up their wrongdoings, the fact that they must rely on the media to draw attention to their antics in the sporting arena means that average citizens can look past the surface level to the underlying problems. When a crime occurs in a country with an authoritarian government—a place where journalists are often targeted for criticizing the authorities—it draws international attention to the situation and provides an opportunity for people to exert pressure on oppressive regimes to loosen up. Sports events can be used by media outlets and NGOs around the world to urge governments to implement socially beneficial reforms. State and local governments can benefit from hosting sporting events, but non-state actors can use these opportunities to "shame" governments—forcing them to take action and make reforms at home. Saudi Arabia, for one, is eager to establish itself as a Western sports powerhouse, yet the world at large is already well aware of the atrocities that have been committed against its own people.

Besides the media and the public, athletes are also often the ones who are questioned about their role in the "success" of sportswashing. They have been attacked by fans for turning a blind eye to any problems that may exist in the teams or competitions they are involved with. While it is true that some athletes choose indifference, we cannot ignore those who choose to rise up and launch their own activism; some go so far as to become "anti-Olympic". It is inevitable that more democracy, accountability, and free speech will emerge as a result of these movements' influence in the sporting world.

Conclusion

The competitiveness of sports games is one of many things that shapes humanity and the way we live—both for the better and the worse. Sports bring people closer, breaking through invisible barriers that we create ourselves. Healthy lifestyles and the sense of friendliness are also the atmosphere that sports want to build to welcome people, no matter of their personal background. As we've already talked about in other chapters, the existence and value of sports help us see our communities and countries as having strong emotional ties that aren't made any other way.

Because of the strong emotional ties that may form between supporters and their favorite teams, leagues, host countries, and players, it's not uncommon for sports fans to turn a blind eye to allegations of wrongdoing when they hear about them. If the government of the country hosting the World Cup or the Olympics is responsible for serious breaches of human rights, our devotion may serve to legitimize the sportswasher even further. So, ordinary people make it easier for the sportswashers to use them to further their political cause.

Many governments will use sporting events to present a new, more approachable image, but they are usually slow to execute substantive reform. Qatar pledged significant reforms to its labor market in response to increased international scrutiny ahead of the World Cup. However, Amnesty International reported that the country is failing to adequately police its labor rules, and that workers continue to be exploited.

However, not everything about sportswashing is negative doom and gloom; for example, the spotlight cast by major sporting events on countries with a history of human rights abuses can increase international pressure on those nations to improve their human rights records and perhaps even prompt them to make positive changes. Even though there seems to be a lot of evidence, the big international groups in charge of sports still deny the existence of sportswashing and reject the claim that their bid decisions are often based on politics and financial gains.

Now, there are big questions to which we don't have a good response: What's next? If supporters play a key role in the sports industry, can we do anything to push back? And, even if there is something we can do, does it mean that we should give up enjoying sports?

The most obvious solution is to stop attending events that are hosted by authoritarian governments. This would use the purchasing power of consumers to encourage international sports federations and organizations like FIFA and the IOC to reconsider their host site selection processes. However, this can be a tall order for sports lovers, who frequently base their hobbies and enjoyment around major sporting events. Ultimately, people's enthusiasm for what happens on the field is too great for them to be worried by what happens off it, making a fan boycott large enough to affect the bottom line of either event highly unlikely.

But if sportswashing is here to stay, we may take action in the sporting world to counter it. One option is to try to get the fan bases of each team to have more control over the teams. This would be similar to the "50+1" system in Germany, which gives the fan bases of each team majority ownership of their teams' sports clubs. However, such a radical change in ownership would be far out of reach due to the financial power the current owners bring to their clubs.

At the end of the day, these are just assertions. Governments, not individuals, are the ones who can make a difference in the world when it comes to human rights issues. However, famous athletes can bring attention to the international community, shedding some light to those who may be unfamiliar with these issues. This is another driving force that is important for creating the political will for change and keeping up the pressure until results are seen.

Sportswashing is based on the premise that spectators will be distracted from human rights abuses by the appeal of glitzy stadiums and famous sports teams. While it's possible we won't be able to wrest complete control of sports back any time soon, players and their supporters still have the capacity to draw attention to human rights abuses and make it so authoritarian governments can't afford to take the risk of even more horrible reputational damage.

Authors Note

T hank you for reading this book!

If you enjoyed it and have a minute to spare, I would really appreciate a short review on the page or site where you bought the book.

Reviews from readers like you really make a huge difference.

Thanks again!

DC

References

Abrams, A. (2022, October 28). *How money is laundered through football*. The Sumsuber. https://sumsub.com/blog/money-laundering-football/

Al-Arian, A. (2022). Opinion | Why the World Cup belongs in the Middle East. *The New York Times.* https://www.nytimes.com/2022/11/18/opinion/qatar-world-cup-arab-football.html

Allison, M., Aswad, Y., & Scott, S. (2022). *FIFA 2022: The benefits for qatar and potential risks*. Leadership and Democracy Lab; Western University. https://www.democracylab.uwo.ca/Archives/2017_2018_research/construction_in_qatar/fifa_2022_the_benefits_for_qatar_and_potential_risks.html

Amnesty International. (2016, June 2). *Brazil on fast-track course to repeat epic World Cup failures during Olympics*. Amnesty International. https://www.amnesty.org/en/latest/press-release/2016/06/brazil-on-fast-track-course-to-repeat-epic-world-cup-failures-during-olympics/

Antunes, A. (2014, May 28). How the 2014 FIFA World Cup became the worst publicity stunt in history.

Forbes. https://www.forbes.com/sites/andersonantunes/2014/05/27/ho
w-the-2014-fifa-world-cup-became-the-worse-publicity-stunt-in-history/

Barber, N. (2016, August 10). *How Leni Riefenstahl shaped the way we
see the Olympics.* BBC. https://www.bbc.com/culture/article/20160810
-how-leni-riefenstahl-shaped-the-way-we-see-the-olympics

Battaglio, S. (2022, December 21). The 2022 World Cup
overcomes obstacles to score a ratings hit. *Los Angeles
Times.* https://www.latimes.com/entertainment-arts/business/story/20
22-12-20/world-cup-final-delivers-26-million-viewers-for-fox

Bensinger, K. (2018, July 16). *When Argentina used World Cup soccer
to whitewash its dirty war.* History. https://www.history.com/news/wor
ld-cup-soccer-argentina-1978-dirty-war

Berkes, H. (2008, June 7). Nazi Olympics tangled politics and sport.
NPR. https://www.npr.org/2008/06/07/91246674/nazi-olympics-tang
led-politics-and-sport

*Birmingham 2022 Commonwealth Games creating a car-
bon neutral legacy.* (n.d.). Commonwealth Games - Birmingham
2022. https://www.birmingham2022.com/about-us/our-purpose/our-le
gacy/sustainability/carbon-neutral-legacy

Bloodworth, A. (2018, June 18). *A philosophical response to the critics of
anti-doping.* Idrottsforum.org; Dept. of Sport Sciences, Malmö University.
https://idrottsforum.org/bloand_murray180618/

Blum, R. (2022, October 14). *Fox will ignore Qatar's human
rights controversy when covering country's soccer World Cup.* Huff-
Post. https://www.huffpost.com/entry/fox-soccer-world-cup-coverage_
n_63493900e4b0e376dc0b6a53

Brison, N. (2022, April 19). *Spotting "greenwashing" in sports.* Global Sport Matters. https://globalsportmatters.com/business/2022/04/19/sports-greenwashing-how-to-spot-it-faq/

Brown, C. (2022, August 22). *Saudi Arabian Sports Minister denies claims of using "sportswashing" ahead of plans to bid for Olympics.* Around the Rings. https://www.infobae.com/aroundtherings/articles/2022/08/22/saudi-arabian-sports-minister-denies-claims-of-using-sportswashing-ahead-of-plans-to-bid-for-olympics/

Bunting, T. (2022, December 2). *"Sporting Democracy" – as illustrated by the Qatar World Cup.* The Loop. https://theloop.ecpr.eu/sporting-democracy-as-illustrated-by-the-qatar-world-cup/

Buschmann, R., Naber, N., & Winterbach, C. (2022, April 7). Manchester City's cozy ties to Abu Dhabi: Sponsorship money – Paid for by the State. *Der Spiegel.* https://www.spiegel.de/international/europe/sponsorship-money-paid-for-by-the-state-a-2ad5b586-1d82-4a21-8065-f3c081cd91a4

Campbell, A. (2017, August 11). Cheating is leeching sport of its magic. In the end, the fans won't stand for it. *The Guardian.* https://www.theguardian.com/commentisfree/2017/aug/11/cheating-sport-magic-fans-corruption-money-drugs

Canniford, R. (2012, October 18). *Greenwash: a critical exposé highlights need for action.* The Conversation. https://theconversation.com/greenwash-a-critical-expose-highlights-need-for-action-10133

Canniford, R., & Hill, T. (2022, January 18). *Sportswashing: How mining and energy companies sponsor your favourite sports to help clean up their image.* The Conversation.

https://theconversation.com/sportswashing-how-mining-and-energy-co
mpanies-sponsor-your-favourite-sports-to-help-clean-up-their-image-173
589

Cascon, M. (2022, March 25). *UFDS annual report: Betting corruption and match-fixing in 2021*. Sportradar. https://sportradar.com/ufds-ann
ual-report/

Chakrabortty, A. (2022, July 21). *How a great English city sold itself to Abu Dhabi's elite – and not even for a good price | Aditya Chakrabortty*. The Guardian. https://www.theguardian.com/commentisfree/2022/jul
/21/great-english-city-sold-abu-dhabis-elite-manchester

Chen, S., & Doran, K. (2022). Using sports to "build it up" or "wash it down": How sportswashing give sports a bad name. *Findings in Sport, Hospitality, Entertainment, and Event Management, 2*(1). https://digita
lcommons.memphis.edu/finsheem/vol2/iss1/3/

Cherry, K. (2013, May). *The halo effect*. Verywell Mind. https://www.
verywellmind.com/what-is-the-halo-effect-2795906

China: Censorship mars Beijing Olympics. (2022, February 18). Human Rights Watch. https://www.hrw.org/news/2022/02/18/china-censorshi
p-mars-beijing-olympics

Chronides, A. (2020, October 7). *The impact of money laun-dering on international sports*. The Sports Financial Literacy Acade-my. https://moneysmartathlete.com/special-themes/the-impact-of-mon
ey-laundering-on-international-sports/

Clarke, M. (2022, February 10). *Can China use the Beijing Olympics to "sportwash" its abuses against the Uyghurs? Only if the world remains silent*. The Conversation.
https://theconversation.com/can-china-use-the-beijing-olympics-to-sport

wash-its-abuses-against-the-uyghurs-only-if-the-world-remains-silent-175
922

Critchlow, A. (2014, August 30). *Manchester City FC have plans for global brand domination.* The Telegraph. https://www.telegraph.co.uk/finance/newsbysector/industry/11065644/ Manchester-City-FC-have-plans-for-global-brand-domination.html

Dart, T. (2022, November 27). *How many migrant workers have died in qatar? What we know about the human cost of the 2022 world cup.* The Guardian. https://www.theguardian.com/football/2022/nov/27/qatar-deaths-how-many-migrant-workers-died-world-cup-number-toll

Draper, K. (2022, November 22). On Fox Sports, viewers get a world cup scrubbed of controversy. *The New York Times.* https://www.nytimes.com/2022/11/22/sports/soccer/fox-sports-world-cup.html

Drugs banned in sport. (2014). Drugs. https://www.drugs com/wada/

Dudley, D. (2022, March 18). *Bahrain's critics push "sports-washing" claim ahead of start of Formula 1 season.* Forbes. https://www.forbes.com/sites/dominicdudley/2022/03/18/bahrains-critics-push-sports-washing-claim-ahead-of-start-of-formula-1-season/

Dufrasne, G. (2022, October 31). *Poor tackling: Yellow card for 2022 FIFA World Cup's carbon neutrality claim – Updated.* Carbon Market Watch. https://carbonmarketwatch.org/publications/poor-tackling-yellow-card-for-2022-fifa-world-cups-carbon-neutrality-claim/

Dunseath, F. (2022, December 12). *Qatar FIFA world cup controversy: What you need to know.* RNZ. https://www.rnz.co.nz/news/what-you-need-to-know/480588/qatar-fifa-world-cup-controversy-what-you-need-to-know

DAVID CARLTON

Dyke, H. (2016, August 8). *Why is doping wrong anyway?* The Conversation. https://theconversation.com/why-is-doping-wrong-anyway-6 3057

Eichberg, H. (2010). Bodily democracy and development through sport - towards intercultural recognition. *Physical Culture and Sport Studies and Research, XLIX.*

"End police brutality", Brazil told ahead of Olympics. (2016, June 3). Al Jazeera. https://www.aljazeera.com/sports/2016/6/3/brazil-urged-to -end-police-brutality-ahead-of-olympics

Enright, D. (2021, October 27). *"Sportswashing" and the Newcastle takeover.* The Oxford Student. https://www.oxfordstudent.com/2021/1 0/27/sportswashing-and-the-newcastle-takeover/

Evans, S. (2022, February 28). UEFA cancel Gazprom sponsorship deal. *Reuters.* https://www.reuters.com/lifestyle/sports/uefa-cancel-gazp rom-sponsorship-deal-source-2022-02-28/

Falkenheim, D., & Prewitt, A. (2022, November 1). *What on earth: How phony environmentalism came to sports.* Sports Illustrated. https://www.s i.com/soccer/2022/11/01/sports-greenwashing-daily-cover

FIFA. (2018, December 21). *More than half the world watched record-breaking 2018 World Cup.* FIFA. https://www.fifa.com/tournaments/mens/worldcup/2018russia/media-r eleases/more-than-half-the-world-watched-record-breaking-2018-world-c up

Ford, M. (2019, May 12). *Saudi sportswashing: Ruiz and Joshua face off in Diriyah.* DW. https://www.dw.com/en/saudi-sportswashing-ruiz-and -joshua-to-face-off-as-rory-mcilroy-turns-down-offer/a-51540942

Fothergill, M. (2022, February 8). *Dizzying highs and crushing lows: is being a sports fan good or bad for you?* The Conversation.

https://theconversation.com/dizzying-highs-and-crushing-lows-is-being-a
-sports-fan-good-or-bad-for-you-176076

Futterman, M. (2022, October 24). Hints of Russians' return to
international sports rekindle debate over their exclusion *The New
York Times*. https://www.nytimes.com/2022/10/24/sports/olympics/pa
ris-russia-ban-ioc.html

Galante, I., & Goldenbaum, C. (2021, September 19). *Five
years on: Revisiting Rio 2016 Olympics' unkept promises*. Al
Jazeera. https://www.aljazeera.com/sports/2021/9/19/five-years-on-revi
siting-rio-2016-olympics-unkept-promises

Garcia-Navarro, L. (2016, August 9). Controversy
grows in Rio over political protests during Olympics.
NPR. https://www.npr.org/sections/thetorch/2016/08/09/489284024
/controversy-grows-in-rio-over-political-protests-during-olympics

Goldman, T. (2022, February 12). "They've ruined it for all
of us," Adam Rippon says of Russia's latest doping scandal.
NPR. https://www.npr.org/2022/02/12/1080338657/olympics-2022-r
ussia-doping-kamila-valieva-adam-rippon

Goldsmith, J. (2022, July 25). *WWE will restate earnings to account
for Vince McMahon's $14.6M "unrecorded payments", warns investors of
current & future probes*. Deadline. https://deadline.com/2022/07/wwe-v
ince-mcmahon-1235076624/

Gulam, A. (2016). Effects of politics on sports. *International Journal of
Multidisciplinary Education and Research*, *1*(9), 61–63. http://www.ed
ucationjournal.in/archives/2016/vol1/issue9/1-10-20

Harrison, S. (2021, July 21). *The "Protest" Olympics that never came to
be*. Smithsonian Magazine. https://www.smithsonianmag.com/history/p
rotest-olympics-never-came-be-180978179/

Hartung, A. (2016, January 23). *Why cheating in sports is prevalent -- and we can't stop it.* Forbes. https://www.forbes.com/sites/adamhartung/2016/01/23/why -cheating-is-prevalent-and-we-cant-stop-it/?sh=2fe32d5ea0e7

Haththotuwa, S. (2022, October 18). *The rise of soft power: can sportswashing be a good thing? - Business Leader News.* Business Leader. https://www.businessleader.co.uk/the-rise-of-soft-power-can-sp ortswashing-be-a-good-thing/

Hough, D. (2022, November 22). *World Cup 2022: heat on Qatar diverts attention from Fifa's failure to tackle proven corruption.* The Conversation. https://theconversation.com/world-cup-2022-heat-on-qatar-dive rts-attention-from-fifas-failure-to-tackle-proven-corruption-194298

How football and "sportswashing" helped Putin start a war. (2022, June 24). DW. https://www.dw.com/en/how-football-and-sportswashing-hel ped-putin-start-a-war/video-62246124

How social issues are shaping sports coverage. (2021, August 11). St. Bonaventure University. https://online.sbu.edu/news/how-social-issues -are-shaping-sports-coverage

ILO-Qatar Technical Cooperation Programme. (2022, November 1). *Four years of labour reforms in Qatar.* International Labour Organization (ILO). https://www.ilo.org/beirut/countries/qatar/WCMS_85988 0/lang--en/index.htm#

Ingle, S. (2022, December 8). *Qatar World Cup chief says "death is a part of life" after reported worker death.* The Guardian. https://www.theguardian.com/football/2022/dec/08/qatar-l aunches-investigation-after-reported-death-of-worker-at-world-cup-site

International Betting Integrity Association, & H2 Gambling Capital. (n.d.-a). An optimum betting market: A regulatory, fiscal & integrity as-

THE HISTORY OF SPORTSWASHING

sessment. In *IBIA*. https://ibia.bet/wp-content/uploads/2021/08/IBIA
-An-Optimum-Betting-Market.pdf

International Betting Integrity Association, & H2 Gambling Capital.
(n.d.-b). An optimum betting market: A regulatory, fiscal & integrity as-
sessment. In *IBIA*. https://ibia.bet/wp-content/uploads/2021/08/IBIA
-An-Optimum-Betting-Market.pdf

International Betting Integrity Association, & H2 Gambling Capital.
(n.d.-c). An optimum betting market: A regulatory, fiscal & integrity as-
sessment. In *IBIA* (p. 74). https://ibia.bet/wp-content/uploads/2021/0
8/IBIA-An-Optimum-Betting-Market.pdf

International Betting Integrity Association, & H2 Gambling Captal.
(n.d.). An optimum betting market: A regulatory, fiscal & integrity assess-
ment. In *IBIA* (p. 74). IBIA. https://ibia.bet/wp-content/uploads/2021
/08/IBIA-An-Optimum-Betting-Market.pdf

IOC Media. (2022). Joint IOC & Beijing 2022 Daily Briefing [Video].
In *Youtube*. https://www.youtube.com/watch?v=jmxSYLJ7JWM

Jesse Owens. (2021, August 3). American Experience PBS. https://www
.pbs.org/wgbh/americanexperience/films/owens/

Jiménez-Martínez, C., & Skey, M. (2018, July 25).
*How repressive states and governments use "sportswash-
ing" to remove stains on their reputation*. The Conversation. https://theconversation.com/how-repressive-states-and-governme
nts-use-sportswashing-to-remove-stains-on-their-reputation-100395

Jones, R. (2023, January 19). *Qatar 2022: World Cup final scores 1.5 bn
global viewers*. SportsPro. https://www.sportspromedia.com/news/qatar
-2022-fifa-world-cup-final-argentina-france-viewers-engagement/

Kamau, R. (2022, March 7). *How football, baseball, and UFC companies
use crypto to build better fan relationships*. Forbes.

https://www.forbes.com/sites/rufaskamau/2022/03/07/sports-deals-are
-helping-crypto-projects-build-communities-and-drive-engagements/?sh
=33b76f231514

Katz, C. (2022, December 19). *From the World Cup to the Olympics: Why are international sporting events so corrupt?* The Global Anticorruption Blog. https://globalanticorruptionblog.com/2022/12/19/from-the-world-cup -to-the-olympics-why-are-international-sporting-events-so-corrupt/

Khabbaz, R. (2021, January 1). *Sports and social justice.* Harvard Business Review. https://hbr.org/2021/01/sports-and-social-justice

Kim, S., & Manoli, A. E. (2022). From horizontal to vertical relationships: How online community identification fosters sport fans' team identification and behavioural intentions. *International Journal of Sports Marketing and Sponsorship.* https://doi.org/10.1108/ijsms-09-2021-0188

King-Hill, S. (2022, November 25). *The Qatar World Cup is beaming misogyny around the world.* The Conversation. https://theconversation.com/the-qatar-world-cup-is-beaming-misogyny-around-the-world-195242

Kurmelovs, R. (2021, November 9). *Fossil fuel advertising in sport "the new cigarette sponsorship", ex-Wallabies captain David Pocock says.* The Guardian. https://www.theguardian.com/business/2021/nov/10/fossil-fuel-advertis ing-in-sport-the-new-cigarette-sponsorship-says-ex-wallabies-captain-davi d-pocock

Kurmelovs, R. (2022, January 22). Tennis Australia ends partnership with Santos after one year. *The Guardian.* https://www.theguardian.com/sport/2022/jan/23/tennis-australia-ends -partnership-with-santos-after-one-year

Kusi, F. A. (2023, February 9). *A conjunct approach in the democratization of sport for development.* Sportanddev. https://www.sportanddev.org /en/article/news/conjunct-approach-democratization-sport-development

Leaver, A., Silver, J., & Goulding, R. (2023, January 9). *Manchester, the centripetal city: The lessons of property-led regeneration for core cities and their proximal towns.* The University of Sheffield. https://www.sheffield. ac.uk/crafic/research/manchester-centripetal-city

Lewis, R. (2022, August 13). *1934 World Cup: The birth of a European footballing giant.* History of Soccer. https://historyofsoccer.info/1934-w orld-cup

López Frías, F. J., & Isidori, E. (2014). Sport and democracy: Philosophical trends and educational challenges in contemporary society. *Cultura, Ciencia Y Deporte, 9*(27), 189–197. https://doi.org/10.12800/ccd.v9i27. 461

Lu, X., Sheng, T., Zhou, X., Shen, C., & Fang, B. (2022). How does young consumers' greenwashing perception impact their green purchase intention in the fast fashion industry? An analysis from the perspective of perceived risk theory. *Sustainability, 14*(20), 13473. https://doi.org/10.3 390/su142013473

Lucas, R. (2011, June 11). *Why does taint of corruption stick to sport and what can we do about it?* The Conversation. https://theconversation.com/why-does-taint-of-corruption-stick-to-sport -and-what-can-we-do-about-it-1578

Mackey, E. (2022, December 5). *2022 world cup records: Which ones have been broken and which could still fall?* The Athletic. https://theathletic.c om/3970548/2022/12/05/records-broken-2022-world-cup/

Malik, K. (2021, June 13). *We need to separate sport and politics. But also recognise they're inseparable.* The Guardian.

https://www.theguardian.com/commentisfree/2021/jun/13/impossible
-to-keep-politics-out-of-sport-just-as-it-should-be

Manchester City exposed: Bending the rules to the tune of millions. (2018, November 5). Der Spiegel. https://www.spiegel.de/international/manchester-city-exposed
-bending-the-rules-to-the-tune-of-millions-a-1236346.html

Match-fixing and gambling in sport. (n.d.). Sport New Zealand | Ihi Aoteroa. https://sportnz.org.nz/resources/match-fixing-and-gamblin
g-in-sport/

McCullough, B. P., Sherry, E., & Bramley, O. (2022, October 27). *Out of bounds: How much does greenwashing cost fossil-fuel sponsors of Australian sport?* The Conversation. https://theconversation.com/out-of-bounds-how-much-does-gree
nwashing-cost-fossil-fuel-sponsors-of-australian-sport-192720

McRae, D. (2022a, April 20). MTK Global, boxing company founded by suspected crime boss Kinahan, folds. *The Guardian.* https://www.theguardian.com/sport/2022/apr/20/boxing-c
ompany-mtk-founded-by-suspected-crime-boss-daniel-kinahan-folds

McRae, D. (2022b, April 21). "A malign influence in boxing": the downfall of Daniel Kinahan. *The Guardian.* https://www.theguardian.com/sport/2022/apr/21/boxing-t
he-downfall-of-daniel-kinahan-malign-influence

Melnæs, H. (2017, March 28). *The slaves of St. Petersburg.* Josimar. https://www.josimar.no/artikler/the-slaves-of-st-petersburg/3851/

Melovic, B., Rogic, S., Cerovic Smolovic, J., Dudic, B., & Gregus, M. (2019). The impact of sport sponsorship perceptions and attitudes on purchasing decision of fans as consumers—relevance for promotion of corporate social responsibility and sustainable practices. *Sustainability*, *11*(22), 6389. https://doi.org/10.3390/su11226389

Michaelson, R. (2021, March 28). *Saudi Arabia has spent at least $1.5bn on "sportswashing", report reveals*. The Guardian. https://www.theguardian.com/world/2021/mar/28/saudi-arabia-has-spent-at-least-15bn-on-sportswashing-report-reveals

Millington, B., & Wilson, B. (2022, June 23). *LIV Golf: Sportwashing vs. the commercial value of public attention*. The Conversation. https://theconversation.com/liv-golf-sportwashing-vs-the-commercial-value-of-public-attention-185478

Morgan, W. J. (2009). Athletic perfection, performance-enhancing drugs, and the treatment-enhancement distinction. *Journal of the Philosophy of Sport, 36*(2), 162–181. https://doi.org/10.1080/00948705.2009.9714755

Næss, H. E. (2018). The neutrality myth: Why international sporting associations and politics cannot be separated. *Journal of the Philosophy of Sport, 45*(2), 144–160. https://doi.org/10.1080/00948705.2018.1479190

Nair, P. (2021, November 21). *Can fans do anything about sportswashing?* UCSD Guardian. https://ucsdguardian.org/2021/11/21/can-fans-do-anything-about-sportswashing/

Nestler, S. (2022, July 17). *War in Ukraine: Which sports have banned athletes from Russia and Belarus?* DW. https://www.dw.com/en/war-in-ukraine-which-sports-have-banned-athletes-from-russia-and-belarus/a-62503336

New report: FIFA's foul play at the 2018 World Cup Russia. (2018, June 7). BWI - Building & Wood Workers' International. https://www.bwint.org/cms/news-72/new-report-fifas-foul-play-at-the-2018-world-cup-russia-1084

Newcastle United takeover: Why did the Saudi-backed bid fail? (2020, July 31). Sky Sports. https://www.skysports.com/football/news/11678/12039480/newcastle-united-takeover-why-did-the-saudi-backed-bid-fail

Newson, M., Buhrmester, M., & Whitehouse, H. (2021). United in defeat: shared suffering and group bonding among football fans. *Managing Sport and Leisure*, 1–18. https://doi.org/10.1080/23750472.2020.1866650

Palek, S. (2015, April 23). *The 1936 Berlin Olympic Games*. Cambridge University Library; University of Cambridge. https://www.lib.cam.ac.uk/collections/departments/germanic-collections/about-collections/spotlight-archive/1936-berlin-olympic

Panja, T. (2019, December 9). Russia banned from Olympics and global sports for 4 years over doping. *The New York Times*. https://www.nytimes.com/2019/12/09/sports/russia-doping-ban.html

Panja, T., & Das, A. (2022, June 10). What is LIV golf? It depends whom you ask. *The New York Times*. https://www.nytimes.com/article/liv-golf-saudi-arabia-pga.html

Panja, T., & Draper, K. (2020, April 6). U.S. prosecutors say Qatar and Russia bribed FIFA officials to win World Cup bids. *The New York Times*. https://www.nytimes.com/2020/04/06/sports/soccer/qatar-and-russia-bribery-world-cup-fifa.html

Panja, T., & Smith, R. (2022, November 19). The World Cup that changed everything. *The New York Times*. https://www.nytimes.com/2022/11/19/sports/soccer/world-cup-qatar-2022.html

Pattisson, P., & McIntyre, N. (2021, February 23). Revealed: 6,500 migrant workers have died in qatar as it gears up for world cup. *The Guardian*. https://www.theguardian.com/global-development/2021/feb/23/revealed-migrant-worker-deaths-qatar-fifa-world-cup-2022

Pattle, A. (2022, August 19). *Boxing looks away from sportswashing accusations ahead of Joshua vs Usyk*. The Independent. https://www.independent.co.uk/sport/boxing/anthony-joshua-usyk-sportswashing-saudi-arabia-b2147864.html

Pearson, M. (2022, June 11). *Opinion: Banners show sportswashing is stalling*. DW. https://www.dw.com/en/opinion-bundesliga-qatar-banners-show-sportswashing-is-stalling/a-63664035

Povich, S. (1996, July 6). *Berlin, 1936: At the Olympics, achievements of the brave in a year of cowardice*. Washington Post. https://www.washingtonpost.com/wp-srv/sports/longterm/general/povich/launch/olympics.htm

Qin, A. (2022, February 8). Bearing an Olympic torch, and a politically loaded message. *The New York Times*. https://www.nytimes.com/2022/02/08/sports/olympics/china-uyghur-olympics.html

Quigley, J. (2016, February 5). 6 months to Rio: 5 controversies looming over the Olympic Games. *CBC News*. https://www.cbc.ca/news/world/rio-olympics-five-controversies-1.3430807

Raji, K. (2022, November 17). *Qatar 2022: The environmental cost of the FIFA World Cup*. Earth. https://earth.org/qatar-2022/

Rappeport, A. (2019, December 2). Saudi Arabia embraces Western sports to rehabilitate global image. *The New York Times*. https://www.nytimes.com/2019/12/02/business/economy/saudi-arabia-image-sports.html

Reade, J. (2023, February 20). *Football finances: what's going on with Manchester City?* Economics Observatory. https://www.economicsobservatory.com/football-finances-whats-going-on-with-manchester-city

Reality check: Migrant workers' rights in Qatar. (2019, February 5). Amnesty Internation-

al. https://www.amnesty.org/en/latest/campaigns/2019/02/reality-chec
k-migrant-workers-rights-with-two-years-to-qatar-2022-world-cup/

Reiche, D. (2016, August 4). Most nations going to the Olympics won't bring home a medal. Here's why they compete anyway. *Washington Post.* https://www.washingtonpost.com/news/monkey-cage/wp/2016/08/04/most-nations-going-to-the-olympics-wont-bring-home-a-medal-heres-wh
y-they-compete-anyway/

Rights groups to Formula 1: Don't "sportswash" Bahrain abuses. (2022, March 16). DAWN. https://dawnmena.org/rights-groups-to-formula-1-dont-sportswash-bahrain-abuses/

Robinson, K. (2022, November 18). *What is the Kafala System?* Council on Foreign Relations. https://www.cfr.org/backgrounder/what-kafal
a-system

Role of sport in modern society cultural studies essay. (2018). UK Essays. https://www.ukessays.com/essays/cultural-studies/role-of-sport-i
n-modern-society-cultural-studies-essay.php

Ronay, B. (2014, January 2). *World Cup 2014: Brazil's horribly invasive footballing trauma.* The Guardian. https://www.theguardian.com/footb
all/2014/jan/02/world-cup-2014-brazil-football-trauma

Rosenberg, M. (2022, December 29). *Sportswashing is everywhere, but it's not new.* Sports Illustrated. https://www.si.com/olympics/2022/12/2
9/sportswashing-olympics-world-cup-daily-cover

Ross, M. (2022, March 8). *Sports are political: Reaction and inaction to Putin's war of aggression.* The Conversation. https://theconversation.com/sports-are-political-reaction-and-inac
tion-to-putins-war-of-aggression-178115

Ruiz, R. R. (2016, May 16). Russian sports doping: Explained. *The New York Times*. https://www.nytimes.com/2016/05/17/sports/olympics/russian-sports-doping-explained.html

Ruiz, R. R., & Schwirtz, M. (2016, May 12). Russian Insider Says State-Run Doping Fueled Olympic Gold. *The New York Times*. https://www.nytimes.com/2016/05/13/sports/russia-doping-sochi-olympics-2014.html

Rybaltowski, M. (2019, December 2). *Analysis of Josh Shaw's ban: Is transparency required from leagues when releasing details on betting investigations?* SportsHandle. https://sportshandle.com/josh-shaw-analysis/

Saucedo, N. (2021, December 17). *Igniting the truth against authoritarian sportswashing.* Human Rights Foundation. https://hrf.org/igniting-the-truth-against-authoritarian-sportswashing/

Sayid, R. (2016, June 14). Falling in love with this sport will cost you more than anything else. *Mirror*. https://www.mirror.co.uk/money/meet-sports-superfans-spending-20billion-8190946

Schmall, T. (2019, January 17). *NFL fans spend 46 hours a month obsessed with their team.* NY Post. https://nypost.com/2019/01/17/nfl-fans-spend-46-hours-a-month-obsessed-with-their-team/

Schneider, R. C., & Stier, W. F. (2008). Leni Riefenstahl's "Olympia": Brilliant cinematography or Nazi propaganda?. *The Sport Journal*. https://thesportjournal.org/article/leni-riefenstahls-olympia-brilliant-cinematography-or-nazi-propaganda/

Shaikhouni, L. (2022, December 14). World Cup 2022: "Finally football smiles back at Arabs." *BBC News*. https://www.bbc.com/news/world-63978847

DAVID CARLTON

Shchedrov, O., & Baldwin, C. (2008, August 6). Drug scandal overshadows Putin's Beijing trip. *Reuters*. https://www.reuters.com/article/us-olympics-doping-russia-idUSSP5172520080806

Skey, M. (2022a). Sportswashing: Media headline or analytic concept? *International Review for the Sociology of Sport*, 101269022211360. https://doi.org/10.1177/10126902221136086

Skey, M. (2022b, December 6). *"Sportswashing": How the washing metaphor evolved beyond the idea of a cover-up*. LSE Business Review. https://blogs.lse.ac.uk/businessreview/2022/12/06/sportswashing-how-the-washing-metaphor-evolved-beyond-the-idea-of-a-cover-up/

Slattery, L. (2018, October 30). *"Sportswashing" is the grim game of our times*. The Irish Times. https://www.irishtimes.com/business/media-and-marketing/sportswashing-is-the-grim-game-of-our-times-1.3679671

Steinberg, J. (2021, October 15). *Match-fixing suspicions raised in 1,100 cases since pandemic's start*. The Guardian. https://www.theguardian.com/sport/2021/oct/15/match-fixing-suspicions-raised-in-1100-cases-since-pandemic-start-sportradar

Stout, J. (2021, July 19). *The brutal story of the 1936 Popular Olympics: a boycott of fascism and Hitler*. National Geographic. https://www.nationalgeographic.com/history/article/brutal-story-1936-popular-olympics-boycott-fascism-hitler

Strauss, B. (2022, November 18). Fox's World Cup coverage of Qatar has a notable sponsor: Qatar. *Washington Post*. https://www.washingtonpost.com/sports/2022/11/18/fox-qatar-world-cup-coverage/

Swinburne University of Technology. (2022, October 27). *Fossil fuel industry using sports to greenwash public image*. Phys.org. https://phys.org/news/2022-10-fossil-fuel-industry-sports-greenwash.html

Tak, M., Sam, M. P., & Jackson, S. J. (2018). The problems and causes of match-fixing: are legal sports betting regimes to blame? *Journal of Criminological Research, Policy and Practice, 4*(1), 73–87. https://doi.org/10.1 108/jcrpp-01-2018-0006

Taylor, M. (2021, March 22). *Major climate polluters accused of greenwashing with sports sponsorship.* The Guardian. https://www.theguardian.com/environment/2021/mar/22/major-climat e-polluters-accused-of-greenwashing-with-sports-sponsorship

The true cost of watching football in the UK revealed. (n.d.). FC Business. https://fcbusiness.co.uk/news/the-true-cost-of-watching-football-i n-the-uk-revealed/

Therapeutic Use Exemptions (TUEs). (n.d.). World Anti-Doping Agency. https://www.wada-ama.org/en/athletes-support-personnel/ther apeutic-use-exemptions-tues

Thiel, A., Villanova, A., Toms, M., Friis Thing, L., & Dolan, P. (2016). Can sport be "un-political"?. *European Journal for Sport and Society, 13*(4), 253–255. https://doi.org/10.1080/16138171.2016.1253322

Towriss, D. (2022, November 24). *Explainer: What is "sportswashing", and how does it threaten democracy?* International Institute for Democracy and Electoral Assistance (International IDEA). https://www.idea.int/blog/explainer-what-%E2%80%98sportsw ashing%E2%80%99-and-how-does-it-threaten-democracy

Treasury sanctions notorious Kinahan organized crime group. (2022, April 11). U.S. Department of the Treasury. https://home.treasury.gov/ news/press-releases/jy0713

Triumph of Hitler: The Berlin Olympics. (2019). The History Place. https://www.historyplace.com/worldwar2/triumph/tr-olympics.htm

2018 FIFA World Cup Russia: In memory of 21 killed workers. (2018). BWI - Building & Wood Workers' International. https://www.bwint.org/cms/news-72/2018-fifa-world-cup-russia-in-memory-of-21-killed-workers-1093

United Nations Office on Drugs and Crime. (2023). *Illegal betting and sport: Global report on corruption in sport.* https://www.unodc.org/documents/corruption/Publications/2022/Global_Report_on_Corruption_in_Sport_Chapter_9.pdf

van der Meij, L., Almela, M., Hidalgo, V., Villada, C., IJzerman, H., van Lange, P. A. M., & Salvador, A. (2012). Testosterone and cortisol release among Spanish soccer fans watching the 2010 World Cup final. *PLoS ONE, 7*(4), e34814. https://doi.org/10.1371/journal.pone.0034814

Wade, S. (2015, January 21). *FIFA is giving Brazil $100 million after the country spent $15 billion on the World Cup.* Business Insider. https://www.businessinsider.com/fifa-is-giving-100-million-to-brazil-after-the-country-spent-15-billion-on-the-world-cup-2015-1

Waldstein, D. (2022, July 29). To 9/11 families, Saudi-backed golf event is "another atrocity." *The New York Times.* https://www.nytimes.com/2022/07/29/sports/golf/liv-trump-september-11.html

Wallace, S. (2022, February 22). Russian warmongering has turned Uefa's reliance on Gazprom money into a no-win nightmare. *The Telegraph.* https://www.telegraph.co.uk/football/2022/02/22/russian-warmongering-has-turned-uefas-reliance-gazprom-money/

Ward, I. (2022, November 19). *The many, many controversies surrounding the 2022 World Cup, explained.* Vox. https://www.vox.com/world/23450515/world-cup-fifa-qatar-2022-controversy-scandals-explained

What legacy will the 2022 world cup leave for qatar? (2023, January 17). Euronews. https://www.euronews.com/2023/01/17/fifa-world-cup-qat ar-2022-what-legacy-will-it-leave-for-qatar

Williams, J. (2022, February 13). *Has Manchester rebuilt London's housing crisis?* Manchester Evening News. https://www.manchestereveningnews.co.uk/news/greater-manc hester-news/manchester-rebuilt-londons-housing-crisis-23083647

Winkel, S. (2008, May 20). *Corruption in sports - it is time to realize anything is possible.* Bleacher Report. https://bleacherreport.com/article s/24405-corruption-in-sports-it-is-time-to-realize-anything-is-possible

Worden, M. (2018, July 13). *Russia's bloody World Cup.* Human Rights Watch. https://www.hrw.org/news/2018/07/13/russias-bloody-world-c up

World Cup 1934 - The story of Mussolini, Italy, and The Blackshirts. (2018, March 11). Pundit Arena. https://punditarena.com/football/the pateam/1934-world-cup-mussolini-italy-fascists/

World Cup 2022: How has Qatar treated stadium workers? (2022, November 9). *BBC News.* https://www.bbc.com/news/world-60867042

World insights: People in Mideast support Qatar World Cup, object Western "racism." (2022, November 25). Xinhua. https://english.news. cn/20221123/8fe72634bbba40e3b485a086418e3535/c.html

Worrall, S. (2016, July 31). *There's a dark history behind the glittering Olympic Games.* National Geographic. https://www.nationalgeographic .com/history/article/olympic-games-history-rio-david-goldblatt

Yakowicz, W. (2022, November 23). *Meet the company policing match-fixing at the World Cup.* Forbes. https://www.forbes.com/sites/willyakowicz/2022/11/23/meet-t he-company-policing-match-fixing-at-the-world-cup/?sh=6210f4935174

DAVID CARLTON

Yee, V., & Specia, M. (2021, January 5). Gulf states agree to end isolation of Qatar. *The New York Times*. https://www.nytimes.com/2021/01/05/world/middleeast/gulf-qatar-blockade.html

Zidan, K. (2022, April 21). *The Kinahan strategy: How the alleged crime lord used boxing and MMA to sportswash his reputation*. Bloody Elbow. https://www.bloodyelbow.com/2022/4/21/23033935/daniel-kinahan-crime-lord-us-sanctions-tyson-fury-mcgregor-mma-boxing-sportswashing-news

About the Author

David Carlton is a child of 1970's and 80's Britain. Growing up in a period of terrorist threats and atrocities developed his keen interest in modern history and investigations into the "why" of global events behind the "what".

An avid sports fan, with a keen interest in not only the action, but the weird, wonderful and more unscrupulous stories from across the world that only sport provides!

David is married, with three children and lives in Bedfordshire, England.

Also By the Author

A History of Irish Organized Crime

Crossing the Line – A History of Sports Cheats, Gamblers and Match Fixing Scandals

Made in the USA
Coppell, TX
28 September 2024

37848412R00085